CREATING SUCCESS

Leadership Strategies
for
Academic Organizations

CREATING SUCCESS

Leadership Strategies for Academic Organizations

by

Wayne Scott, Ph.D.
with T. Frank Hardesty

Copyright © 2000 by Wayne Scott, Ph. D.

All rights reserved.
No part of this book may be reproduced, stored in a retrieval system, or transmitted by any means, electronic, mechanical, photocopying, recording, or otherwise, without written permission from the author.

ISBN: 1-58820-132-5

1stBooks - rev. 11/14/00

*The authors are aware
that both men and women are employed in leadership
positions in academic organizations. However,
in most cases, masculine pronouns are used in the
text of this book. The
authors ask that when masculine pronouns such
as he, him and other are
used that the reader consider them to be representative
of both genders.*

MEMORANDUM

TO: Users of the book, <u>Creating Success: Leadership Strategies for Academic Organizations</u>

FROM: Wayne Scott, Ph.D.

SUBJECT: Creating Your Own Success

Have you ever wished you were two . . . or maybe three people? That top management would be more impressed with your leadership flair and ideas? That you could leave at the end of the day knowing that you're on top of the workload?

Now there's help!

<u>Creating Success</u> goes, point-by-point, over all those routine, day-in-day-out operations you'd love to speed up and improve... and shows you how to speed up and improve them. From time management to implementing an individual management by objectives program.

The authors of this unique book have devoted years to in-depth study of leadership development. What they've created. . . and you'll have the opportunity of discovery . . . is a completely new approach to personal development.

No blue sky . . . no fancy psychological theories. You'll get practical how-to's that help make the most of your working day.

You won't sit still for a minute once you start this book. You'll write reports, memos, job objectives, and motivational job descriptions . . . and practice speech making.

At the end of having studied this book you will have acquired a wide range of new ideas that you can put to immediate use.

For example:

- TIME MANAGEMENT - save more than two hours a day

- COMMUNICATIONS - add extra power to your speaking and writing

- PLANS FOR ACTION - develop concrete goals and ways to achieve them

- CREATIVITY - stimulate your thinking and spark new ideas

You'll find out how to increase communications in your college or university with a one-sheet five-minute-per-week report.

You'll see how your own increased efficiency can, in turn, make those who work with you and for you more productive.

Take a look at the contents of this book. There is no base left untouched. Most phases of your job are covered **in detail . . . with sound methods of controlling time . . . improving internal communications . . . upgrading** productivity in your organization. Most important, however, you will have created your own success and contributed to the success of others in your academic organization.

CONTENTS

Memorandum From Wayne Scott vii

CHAPTER

1. Individual Organization 1

2. Turn Dreams Into Progress 15

3. Poor (?) Man's PERT 27

4. Make Ideas Make Progress 43

5. More Meetings, More Progress 59

6. Time Management 73

7. Someone Should Do Something About Communications Around Here 89

8. The Administrator's Professional Bibliography 99

9. How to Make An Eloquent Speech 109

10. How to Write A Policy 119

11. How to Assert Authority 133

12. How to Hack A Way Out of the Clerical Jungle 145

x

Chapter 1

Individual Organization

"Organizing your area of control. . . Organizing your future . . . Applying the Present-Future 1-2 Punch"

INTRODUCTION: Stancey Unnorris, President, Unnorris College, glowered. He glowered at Bubiel Nonsmith, Management Consultant. "Nonsmith, you wouldn't have gotten in here in the first place . . . except for that trick calling card of yours. What's this business of just sending in a computer punch card with your last name scrawled on the back? Hard to read, too."

In all respect, Dr. Unnorris, I did get in.

"True. And fair enough. But I don't think you'll be here long."

Didn't plan to be here long, Dr. Unnorris. We're both too busy for long, friendly visits.

"Look, Nonsmith . . . you're proposing to me a way to organize myself and my college. Right?"

Right.

"Well, do you have any idea of how many pieces of mail I get . . . every day. . . giving me magic answers on 'Organization'?"

Quite a few, I expect. I get quite a few myself.

"And your approach is different?"

Different, yes. But more important, my approach works. It will allow your college to progress into the future.

Stancey Unnorris, President, Unnorris College, beamed. He beamed at Bubiel Nonsmith, Management Consultant. "Nonsmith, you just said the magic word . . . progress. Now . . . tell me your story."

All right, Dr. Unnorris. Here's the approach. The problem with people who think "organization" is that they think of it as an end. It isn't. Organization is a means to an end. That end is progress.

Another problem with the thought of organization is this: People think organization is one-dimensional. Too many people view organization as a group of happy hewers of wood and carriers of water . . . singing as they work . . . secure in their fringe benefits and warm under the wing of tenure, or whatever hierarchy.

Above organization are seen those removed from it because of their high level. Its exceptions. Those who control the work. Its presidents. Vice Presidents. Deans.

In truth, no one on the college payroll is outside of or above organization. All are within it. And when organization is three-dimensional, all prosper by being part of it. Organization doesn't limit, doesn't hold back. Organization frees and motivates people- when it is three-dimensional. These are the three dimensions:

1. Organizing your area of control
2. Organizing your future
3. Applying the present-future 1-2 punch

1.1 ORGANIZING YOUR AREA OF CONTROL

Most job descriptions aren't worth their file space. Certainly they are not worth the staggering fee of the consultant who, locked in an impenetrable ivory tower, wrote them. No two people even seem to have quite the same answer to the question: "What is the purpose of having written job descriptions?"

"So . . . what is the answer?"

Good question, Dr. Unnorris. How about the answer being: The purpose of written job descriptions is to make progress.

"Fair enough. But too general. Be more specific."

Okay. A job description will make progress when it motivates people to do better work and to do more work . . . and I mean more productive and creative work. Also, a job description doesn't cause productivity and creativity when it merely expresses a man's limits (too many job descriptions do this) . . . and is progress-causing when it lives and breathes as a document that gives a man more freedom than he'd have without a job description.

To motivate a man, his job description must be "his baby." In other words, his job description must be "birthed" by him. After the birth, superiors may add to and subtract from and make adjustments to that job description. A man will sit still for that, because the original product was his. A man will not sit still for the job description someone else writes and hands to him with the never-spoken but clearly implied result: "Here's your bag. Carry it."

"Sounds okay. But how does this thing get started? What must happen? I'm a little weary and out of patience with people who tell me what to do and don't, and probably can't, tell me how. How? That's my question."

All right. Take a look at Figure 1-1. It's a simple one-sheet form requiring seven entries. Let's use as an example a college with a president, three vice presidents, four deans reporting to each vice president, seven department heads reporting to each dean. Probably no college is structured just that way but, by using that organization as a frame of

1.
2.
3.
4.
5.
6.
7.

Figure 1-1. Present Job Description

reference, an administrator can hammer the concept into his own college's organization, be it five or fifty thousand people.

So the president calls in his three vice presidents. "Gentlemen," he says, "here is a form. I will appreciate your filling in the form, with your own words, to describe what you feel are the seven most important responsibilities you have to this college."

"But," will protest a vice president, "we already have written job descriptions. Isn't this a duplication?"

"Probably not," will answer the president. "My experience is that a job description rarely pictures what a man really does. I want to know what a man gets out of a job, not what he puts into it."

"But, why seven?" will ask a vice president. "Might not five, six, eight or nine sometimes be right?"

"Yes. Seven likely won't hold up under all the battling we'll be doing until we all agree on what you guys are up to. But seven is where we start. I'll tell you why: If you ask a person to write down his responsibilities, the insecure man will write you a book . . . and the lazy man will scrawl a few words on the back of an old envelope. You'll end up with apples and oranges. But when you ask a man to write his seven major responsibilities . . . he will, in his intelligence, arrange to comprise a good 95% of his job. I'll take 95%. I can run a college on that, and you can run a department on that."

The listing of responsibilities will be returned quickly. The job is quite easy . . . at first. The president will look over the forms. He'll be shocked at (1) the fact that this listing is far a field from those aging and yellowed job descriptions in the personnel file (2) the number of duplications . . . and, in responsibilities, there must be no duplications (3) the number of listings with which he disagrees.

So the president triggers a series of discussions with his vice presidents. In those discussions, adjustments to responsibilities are made. In reasonable time, the three vice presidential listings are in final form. As an example, the vice president of administration may now have a listing similar to Figure 1-2.

At this point, each vice president duplicates the previous activities with his deans. In reasonable time they too have birthed and firmed up their listings or responsibilities (perhaps seven or five or six or eight or eleven or whatever, in final form). Then each dean goes the same route with the department heads. Result: 99 written job descriptions, as birthed by each individual . . . and as hammered into reality by their communications with each other. Ninety-nine people now motivated, in a very real sense, to do what they said they will do. The college, the division, the department . . . or any definable area of control . . . is legitimately organized.

1.2 ORGANIZING YOUR FUTURE

Many a college is missing out on a progress patch that is easily cultivated. Having used (rightly or wrongly) job descriptions to picture the way things should be done . . . colleges don't follow through to organize the way things should be done at some selected future point in time.

"A job description for the future. Sounds interesting. I'd really like to hear the 'how' on that one. Is there a how . . . or is this a pipe dream cooked up in our friendly neighborhood business college?"

No pipe dream. And surely not from a business college, which is still mainly teaching the way business was done yesterday. Yes, there's a how on it. Here it is:

After your people have completed their responsibilities listings, they now know how to follow the routines of listing, arguing, adjusting. So . . . duplicate the routines, with one exception. Use the future as the base. Action begins when the president calls his people together for a brief meeting. In general terms, the president describes where he wants the college to go, what he wants the college to do in, say, the next three years (could be three years, five years, whatever time he likes).

Then, the president asks people involved for listings on the 7-responsibilities form as shown in Figure 1-3. The listings cover the responsibilities they see in their jobs three years hence. When these listings are received, adjustments are made in accordance with the college direction. The result: The 99 key people all have two job descriptions . . . present and future. Each knows where he is and where he is going. The benefit: The people aren't driving the college by only looking through the rear-view mirror. Now there's a windshield. Clean windshield, too.

1.3 APPLYING THE PRESENT-FUTURE 1-2 PUNCH

The future job description describes, for every individual, a better job than does the present job description. That better job will pay more money. It lists heavier responsibilities and new areas of operation.

1. Supervising institutional research activities and projects
2. Working with all areas of the college to gain their counsel during all stages of planning and construction of college facilities
3. Coordinating the preparation of local and state M&O and capital outlay budgets
4. Developing and recommending administrative and financial policies and procedures, and coordinating the implementation and exercise of all policies and procedures
5. Maintaining accurate personnel records for all college employees
6. Supervising the design and updating of a college information center through the central administrative data processing function
7. Providing and supervising an administrative accounting and reporting system to support the management of the college

Figure 1-2. Present Job Description

These new areas of operation require the acquisition of more education, new skills.

Every administrator knows that, if he is to advance, he must gain more education and develop new skills. But, without a future job description, he can't be quite sure of exactly what education, what skills. So . . . many people do nothing about the future. Many worry, because they know they should be doing something. So they look for a person to blame. He is easy to find. He is the boss.

"I'm a good man," is the complaint. "Why doesn't my boss be a boss? Why doesn't he talk to me? Why doesn't he tell me what the college has in mind for me? Why doesn't he recommend the courses I should take, the skills I should learn?"

Perhaps those questions should be answered by the boss. But the lead-off statement "I'm a good man" is open to serious doubt. Good men don't wait for someone else to draw their road maps to advancement for them, to hold their hand, to give them a pat on the popo and a lollipop. A good man will write his own two job descriptions. A good man will see to it that he fills his present job description better than anyone else.

A good man will identify, from his future job description, what he must learn in order to cut that future mustard. A good man will learn what he must know. A good man will complete Figure 1-4 and use it to attain success. But . . . "a good man is hard to find."

Key people in colleges which use the double job description concept are unerringly directed. With even a minimum of cooperation among all levels, any individual can move through the education and training that will assure his progress. All won't, of course. But some will. All those who do advance in this fashion will make for one heck of a college or university.

1.
2.
3.
4.
5.
6.
7.

Figure 1-3. Future Job Description

Each year the two job descriptions are re-written. Updated. Thus, as time goes by and men progress, each continues to look ahead as he follows directions that will never quite reach perfection . . . but where the effort is always fun and always progress-causing.

1.4 THE ACHIEVING ACTION

Most colleges won't consider the double job description concept. It is new. Different. Most colleges will want to copy someone else's success . . . or fancied success. But any individual who would succeed can begin his own personal and private double job description program. He may do this right now . . . today. If he does, he'll be better off than if the college had adopted the plan.

Because he'll be the only man with two job descriptions, he will clobber his competition. He will move ahead as far as he wants to go.

And for five years, that's as far as his future job description says he will go. And the three years after that. And the three after that. And . . .

NIGHT SCHOOL COURSES NEEDED				
Description	Date Begins	Date Ends	Cost	Results Expected

CORRESPONDENCE COURSES NEEDED				
Description	Date Begins	Date Ends	Cost	Results Expected

BOOKS NEEDED		
Title	Cost	Results Expected

EXPERIENCE NEEDED				
Description	Where Available	Date Start	Estimated Length	Results Expected

Figure 1-4. Education and Experience Program

SUCCESS EXERCISES

After having studied Chapter 1 you should be able to:

(1) Write your "present" job description
(2) Write your "future" job description
(3) Plan an individual "education and experience program" for your future job

1-1 Using a copy of Figure 1-1, write the seven most important things you do on your job. Don't be too concerned with grammar . . . you can work on that later.

1-2 Go to the individual to whom you report in your organization. Give him the piece of paper which you have just completed titled PRESENT JOB DESCRIPTION. Tell him these are the seven most important things you are "up to" . . . Ask for his comments. Expect some argument. Remember all progress is born of friction; consequently, a few changes may occur. Having completed this activity, you now have a good base of communications. Both you and the person to whom you report know what you are "up to."

1-3 Using a copy of Figure 1-3, write the seven most important things you will do in the future on your present job. Look ahead a bit . . . three years or maybe four or five. You be the judge. How do you see your present job at such time? Let your imagination roam. Some of the things on your future job description will be the same as your present job description. Some will not, because you will have made some things happen that will cause your job to change.

1-4 Go to the individual to whom you report in your organization. Give him the piece of paper which you have just completed titled FUTURE JOB DESCRIPTION. Tell him these are the seven most important things you will be up to in the future on your job. Tell him you think this is what your job will be in three or four years. Expect some changes as before. When you leave your boss's office you will have two important pieces of paper. And they are mighty important. One says what you are up to and the second says this is the way things are going to be. You now have a road map consistent with your college's goals.

1-5 Complete a copy of Figure 1-4. As you do, ask yourself these questions: What do I need to know? What books do I need to read? What experiences do I need to do well on my future job? Be tough on yourself; be very specific . . . because these experiences will exist as the base for your personal success.

Chapter 2

Turn Dreams Into Progress

"A college administrator should let his imagination soar . . . then engineer it back to earth. What a mediocre man calls a 'limitation' is merely a 'ground rule' to the winner."

"The Winner's Club is open to new members. Any color. Any age. Any sex. The dues are effort. This chapter sets forth the ground rules that make those efforts effective."

INTRODUCTION: "Management by Objectives" is a much used term. Many books have been written about the subject. Many articles. Lots of speeches are made . . . mainly by men with deep voices who tell what must be done and never seem to get around to telling how to do it.

"Management by Objectives" too often comes forth as part of a Management-Development Program" . . . produced by someone who never managed anything, and whose development was arrested in the university library.

There is no such thing as "management development." There is only "self development." When men develop themselves, then management becomes their natural habitat. Management is a good place to live . . . and the simple stark reality of true "Management by Objectives" will help get a man to management level and keep him there. He must climb three steps:

1. Dream up a gaggle of objectives
2. Establish the five major objectives
3. Maintain the five major objectives

2.1 DREAM UP A GAGGLE OF OBJECTIVES

"Gaggle" really is a word. It describes a group of geese. Not any group of geese, though. For example . . . when geese are flying ("on the wing," one might say), they are a "skein." Flying geese are a "skein of geese."

But when geese are on the water, they are not a skein. On the water, they are a "gaggle" of geese.

Now . . . objectives may indeed be "on the wing." When they are "in process," perhaps they are a "skein of objectives." But at this point one is dealing with objectives in their birthing stage. When they haven't yet "taken off." Thus, a "gaggle of objectives."

Stancey Unnorris, President, Unnorris College, stared across his desk. He stared at L. Patrick Semicut, Dean of the College. . . "L. Patrick . . . you have two job descriptions . . . Right?"

Right, Dr. Unnorris.

"You have your 'present job description' and your 'future job description.' Right?"

Yes. I have both.

"Okay. Now do this. Go away and study both job descriptions. Ask yourself: What must I do to fill my present job description to perfection . . . and to be ready to make my future job description work? When you do this, many, many answers will flood your mind. As they do, write them down on a form as shown in Figure 2-1."

"Just write them down as the thoughts occur. Forget syntax. Frankly, I don't like anything that ends in 'tax' . . .

but everything seems to. Anyway, you'll be surprised at the number of thoughts that will come from your mind. A hundred, maybe. I've talked to people who generated over three hundred. But . . . write them all down. Okay?"

Okay.

"Stop when your mind 'runs out of gas.' You will then have written down all your thoughts about how you feel this college can prosper. Got it?"

Got it.

"After you've written down your ideas . . . let's wade through those mental products and get your best thinking."

2.2 ESTABLISH FIVE MAJOR OBJECTIVES FROM YOUR IDEAS

"Scan all your ideas, L. Patrick. Make check marks against the more important ones. Then make another check mark against those which you feel are of more importance than the others. Keep selecting and choosing until you end up with the five most important of those thoughts. Are you with me?"

With you, Dr. Unnorris.

"Then let's make objectives out of those random thoughts."

How?

"By quantifying them, L. Patrick. By wording them in such a way that, every day of your life, you can look at your five major objectives and know how you've done lately."

Sounds right. Can you give me an example, Dr. Unnorris?

"Sure. Let's say that one of your thoughts was, 'Let's reduce the failure rate in English 101.' Is that a good one?"

Figure 2-1. Random Ideas

Sure is. It'll certainly be on my list.

Stancey Unnorris paused and lit his pipe. He had read an article which put forth that, to be impressive, one should create the electric pause that goes with pipe-lighting. The same article declared that if one had a piercing glare (Stancey had watery blue eyes, and did fancy himself as a man with a piercing glare), one would be most impressive when glaring through pipe smoke. So Stancey Unnorris glared through pipe smoke and said to L. Patrick Semicut:

"Anyone would agree with that. Wanting to reduce the failure rate in English 101 is like being for motherhood. Everyone agrees. Or against sin . . . most categories. Everyone agrees. But now let's quantify. Let's ask, of your thoughts . . . and this example in particular . . . exactly where must I go, from what point, by what time. Wouldn't you say that was specific?"

L. Patrick coughed. Pipe smoke. Also, he was climbing the walls. He was in day number three of his latest "stop smoking" campaign (largely due to the fierce nagging and inexorable television research of his righteously non-smoking spouse), and breathing smoke invoked fond and recent memories of what L. Patrick had by now rationalized into a harmless vice. In short, day number four would never dawn. He replied: "I would, yes. I would say that was specific."

"Then your thought, in order to qualify as an objective would perhaps be written: 'TO INCREASE THE PERCENTAGE OF STUDENTS PASSING ENGLISH 101 FROM 54 PERCENT TO 72 PERCENT OF THE YEAR'S TOTAL BY JUNE 1, 20XX."

"Now you have a carrot in front of your nose. An acceptable carrot. Because, while a man will resent someone else lining up objectives for him . . . he will gladly respond to the pressure of his own avowed purpose. Isn't that pretty much the way people are?"

I'd say so, Dr. Unnorris. There are, it occurs to me, many males in colleges. More males than men. You have described the way a man thinks. I believe I'm in that class.

"So do I. Now prove it. Select your five most important thoughts.

Quantify them into living objectives. Write all five down on a form such as shown in Figure 2.2."

"Place that completed form on your desk, where you can see and check, every day of your life, what you are doing versus what you said you were going to do."

Okay. I'll do it. Tell me, Dr. Unnorris . . . do you want to approve my objectives?

Pause. "Approve?" Pause and puff. "Not exactly. I'd like to see them, L. Patrick. I'd like to fuss with you a little bit about them. Might be able to be of some help. But, approve? I don't think so. I can't imagine your conjuring up an objective of which I'd disapprove. Let's say I'd like to discuss your five objectives with you, when you're ready."

That'll be tomorrow, Dr. Unnorris.

"My door will be open, L. Patrick."

And they were written. And they were fussed over. And they were re-written. And they were good. And L. Patrick Semicut bought a carton of cigarettes.

2.3 MAINTAIN FIVE MAJOR OBJECTIVES AT ALL TIMES

Some objectives will change while in process. Because conditions do change. When this happens, the Administrator will change his wording . . . but not his resolve. He will continue to progress until the objective, in whatever form, is attained. When that objective is attained, he will replace it with another. For all his life, he will be working toward five quantified and progressive objectives.

Some objectives will change. Complete turnaround from good to useless. Because conditions do change. When this happens, the Administrator will "retire" the out-of-phase objective and will replace it with a new one. He won't waste time complaining because education has (and education is people) changed. People do change . . . education with them. His new objective will make a "full five" . . . and he will, for all his life, be working toward five quantified and progressive objectives.

Some objectives will be right but the administrator will be wrong. In short, he will fail. When he does, he won't waste time looking for someone else to blame (even though someone else may well be to blame). He'll shrug off his failure with a new objective. His new objective will make a "full five" . . . and he will, for all his life, be working toward five quantified and progressive objectives.

Some objectives will be right and the administrator will be right and the hard fight from thought to result will be fought well and won hands down. And that . . . is what the life of an administrator is all about. That is his kick. His thrill. The mahoskus.

When this success is gained, the administrator has been known to take off and get a nose full of booze. His actions at this time of the full crest of success may be unbecoming to the beady eye of the mediocre man. His spouse is not too pleased, either . . . especially if he gave up giving up smoking.

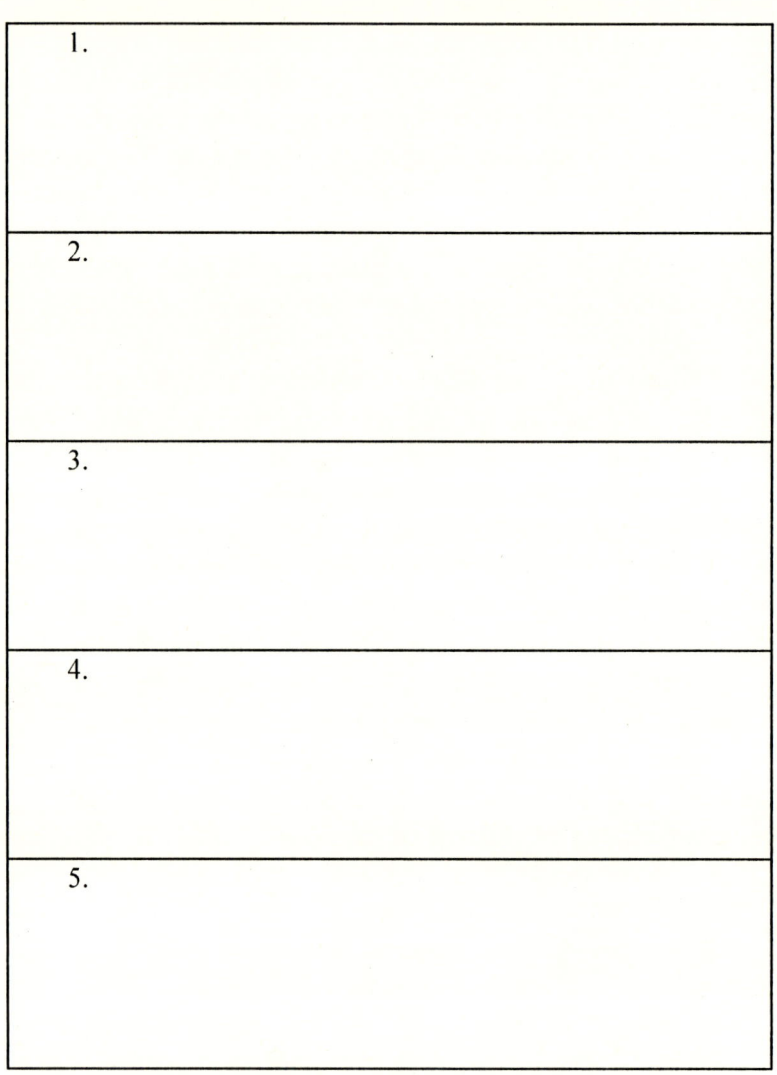

Figure 2-2. Five Quantified Objectives

But the administrator wastes little time in wet triumph. He is soon back at a new starting post. He lists another objective. This new objective will make a "full five" . . . and he will, for all his life, be working toward five quantified and progress-causing objectives.

2.4 THE ACHIEVING ACTION

All objectives, merely because they are quantified, listed and assiduously pursued, do not end up as "dreams come true." For each that doesn't, 1X is taken out of a man. But some objectives are dreams come true. And when he hits, success adds 100X to the administrator. Balances and exceeds a lot of single X's.

The objective-oriented administrator is something like Antaeus. Antaeus was a bad guy in mythology, and Hercules was sent to slay him. Problem was: Earth was the mother of Antaeus. So . . . every time Hercules smacked Antaeus down, Antaeus was given more strength by Mother Earth.

So Antaeus would rise and fight better. Hercules saw no future in this, so he activated an idea. He held Antaeus above the ground and slew him.

Yes, the objective-oriented administrator is like Antaeus. Somewhat. He's not a bad buy, but his strength is replenished when he gets a setback. And nobody will hold this winner above the ground. Because he's a heavyweight, with his feet firmly planted.

Those feet will stay firmly planted. He won't.

SUCCESS EXERCISES

After having studied Chapter 2 you should be able to:

1. List "progress-causing random ideas"
2. Make "quantified objectives" from your ideas
3. Implement a simple and effective individual "Management by Objectives" program that will play an important part in your success

1-1 Using a copy of Figure 2-1, exercise your "relevant creativity" by listing random ideas. These random ideas should relate to making the place where you toil a better place. They should be ideas that are capable of making progress for your college. More than likely you already have some written in the margins of notes taken at meetings . . . Or stored ideas that were generated in the middle of your most recent "crisis."

A sure way of triggering your relevant creativity is to take a copy of Figure 2-1 to the privacy of your office (or your home). Ask yourself the question, "WHAT MUST HAPPEN ON MY JOB TO MAKE IT GO BETTER THAN IT GOES?"

1-2 Return to your completed RANDOM IDEAS. It is now your task to select the five most important ideas on your list. Which ideas are the most urgent? Place a circled one by the most urgent idea. Next place a circled two by the second most urgent idea. Continue until you have your five most important (urgent) ideas for making your job go better.

1-3 You are now ready to convert your five most important and urgent random ideas into "QUANTIFIED OBJECTIVES."

To quantify a random idea write it down in such a way that it is specific. Random ideas are not specific. As an example, suppose your random idea had been "Let's reduce the failure rate in English 101." In order to quantify as an objective this may be written: "TO INCREASE THE PERCENTAGE OF STUDENTS PASSING ENGLISH 101 FROM 54 PERCENT TO 72 PERCENT OF THE YEAR'S TOTAL BY JUNE 1, 20XX.

Rules which will aid in writing quantified objectives are:

1. Always start your objective with the word TO
2. Follow the word TO with a verb, e.g., INCREASE
3. Next is the what of the objective, e.g., THE PERCENTAGE OF STUDENTS PASSING ENGLISH 101
4. The criterion is the next part, e.g., FROM 54 PERCENT TO 72 PERCENT OF THE YEAR'S TOTAL
5. Final quantification is achieved with the stipulation of the time necessary to accomplish the objective, e.g., BY JUNE 1, 20XX

Now you are ready to quantify ideas. Using a copy of Figure 2-2, convert your five most important and urgent ideas into "QUANTIFIED OBJECTIVES."

1-4 Go to the person to whom you report in your college. Show him your five quantified objectives. Tell him these are the five most important things you are up to. He should be impressed because most people don't know what their five objectives are and you do. Sit down and talk together. You will argue. He will say, "Gee, I like this one and this one looks pretty good." But he is going to find one he doesn't like . . . "Don't want to do that one," he'll say. Argument will then occur and some changes will be made. When you leave his office what you have will not be what you had when you went in. But what you have, and you may be the only one in your college that has it, is a piece of paper and on that piece of paper are the five most important things you are up to. And most important, you have the agreement of the person to whom you report.

1-5 Place your random ideas and five quantified objectives in a ring binder. Begin to work immediately on your objectives. When an objective is completed, then recycle. Pick the next most important idea and convert it to a quantified objective.

Everyday of your life you will be working on five quantified objectives. And, Oh! Boy! . . . will you be motivated because you had a part in developing the objectives.

1-6 Have the people who report to you complete these exercises. Soon everyone will have five quantified objectives . . . and Oh! Boy! . . . will they be motivated.

Chapter 3

Poor (?) Man's PERT

"Understand the Progress Magic of Poor Man's PERT . . . Quickly Learn Poor Man's PERT . . . Activate and Progress From Poor Man's PERT."

INTRODUCTION: Lively and curious minds search endlessly for better ways to do things.

When this searching is successful, society benefits from the resulting inventions of products and techniques. In the area of planning techniques, new approaches have been so numerous that it has been difficult to separate the good ones from the great ones.

As a consequence, one management tool developed by the U.S. Navy, which is the greatest planning device of all time, has gone all but unnoticed by most college administrators. That device is PERT. "PERT" means Program Evaluation and Review Technique . . . a descriptive title best forgotten, in that, even if it does hold a degree of accuracy, it does not mirror the great concept that it is.

In its pure form, PERT is an approach by which planners can, on paper, list tasks to be performed in order to meet a goal. PERT's unique discipline is such that it literally forces planners to reap these benefits:

1. No task will be overlooked. All will be listed.
2. The PERT network tells when certain tasks should begin and end. . . and which can be done concomitantly.

3. The PERT network is itself a perfect follow-up document. It gives control to the man in charge . . . enables him to spot and solve problems in early stages.

So, if PERT is all this good, why hasn't its use been more widespread? If PERT is the greatest planning device of all time, then why isn't it being used as such? Why, indeed, have many college administrators never even heard of PERT . . . and, of those who have, why have very few actually ever seen a PERT network?

PERT has not had widespread use because it was devised, and is still largely used for huge and complex projects. Building a ship, for example, or building an apartment house. Until recently, the concept of PERT has not been simplified and presented for use by college administrators whose needs are more in the areas of projects and procedures which number twenty or thirty steps (or less) . . . than in the areas of vast projects of thousands of steps.

Today, there are a number of simplified PERT approaches. They all work. They all profit the man who learns and activates. The approach presented here is the simplest of all. Its title of "Poor Man's PERT" does not mean that the approach is for poor college administrators. It does mean that the difference in progress generated, before and after learning and activating Poor Man's PERT, will be enough to make the user think, in comparison, that he was indeed poor before he benefited from Poor Man's PERT.

The college administrator who would benefit from Poor Man's PERT will take three steps. They are:

1. Understand the Progress Magic of Poor Man's PERT
2. Quickly Learn Poor Man's PERT
3. Activate and Progress From Poor Man's PERT

3.1 UNDERSTAND THE PROGRESS MAGIC OF POOR MAN'S PERT

When a college administrator decides to perform an action, he can never take that action as a single step. Not even if he is a one-man college. Not if he works for Slippery Rock or Ohio State. And not if his college is any size in between.

Every action taken has three parts, as described in an old and dependable engineering principle. Those three parts to any action are (1) Make Ready, (2) Do and (3) Put Away. This principle applies to action ranging in complexity from building a new campus all the way down to making a telephone call.

For example, a telephone call isn't simply made in one step. The "Make Ready" is to determine the phone number and dial the phone. The "Do" is the telephone dialogue itself. The "Put Away" is the action taken as a result of the call.

So it is that all administrative actions follow procedures. Mostly, the procedures are simple enough that there is no need to put them in writing. Let's put it this way: It would not be advisable to give a college president written instructions on how to make his phone calls.

On the other hand, one of the colleges' major weaknesses is not having written procedures in cases where there should be written procedures . . . be they write-ups or repetitive functions such as purchasing, employment, course change approvals or single-shot major projects such as building a second campus, etc. The single outstanding reason why written procedures do not exist or, where they do, are scattered about in memo form or have not been updated since the cotton gin changed things around is because college administrators have decided that the writing of procedures is an expensive task which can be done only by engineers or, perish the thought, outside consultants.

Wrong. Dead wrong. Written procedures are needed, are progress-causing and are available to college administrators through the practical magic of Poor Man's PERT . . . at a cost so small as to be considered zero. Available, too, is control of major projects, where Poor Man's PERT stands forth as the answer to the dilemma of delegation . . . the answer of how to delegate and control.

And once the college administrator has activated Poor Man's PERT and has obtained the procedures he wants and has tasted success on his delegated projects . . . he will find so many other uses for this remarkable concept that he'll wonder how, in the past, he ever got along without it.

3.2 QUICKLY LEARN POOR MAN'S PERT

If an administrator gets a good look at a PERT network, as applied to a complex project, he'll be inclined to take off at high port and never get near another. Because he will have seen a twenty-foot long sheet jammed full of circles, arrows, squiggles, numbers and comments which, on any first look, would be enough to give pause to anyone.

But college administrators don't usually involve themselves with the painful details of vast projects. Their need is to efficiently get students registered . . . to improve instruction . . . to operate within the budget . . . and so on. The college administrator will probably never need to know PERT in its pure form . . . but he does need Poor Man's PERT, and here are his rules for attacking a problem (we'll use, for our example, TO DEVELOP A PUBLIC RELATIONS PLAN IN WRITTEN FORM FOR THE APPROVAL OF THE ADMINISTRATIVE CABINET BY JULY 1, 20XX):

1. Use the Poor Man's PERT form of Figure 3-1.

2. In the "WHAT" column, write a description of any step of the procedure.

NOTE: One of the reasons why people do not write procedures, or make written plans for major projects, is because they don't know where to start. One advantage of Poor Man's PERT is this: It isn't at all necessary to know where to start. Start anywhere. PERT's discipline will make things come out properly.

OBJECTIVE OR PROCEDURE:			
PERT NO.	CHRON. NO.	WHO	WHAT

Figure 3-1. Poor Man's PERT

3. In the "WHO" column, write the title of the person who will perform the "What" as described.

4. In the "PERT NUMBER" column, write the figure "100."

5. Then ask yourself two questions: (1) What must happen before this? (2) What must happen after this?

6. Answer one of the above questions and write the step on the form. If the task happens before #100, assign it a number lower than 100. If the task happens after #100, assign it a higher number in the PERT No. column.

7. Continue this process until you run out of answers to your two questions, as applied to every task. At this point, the procedure (or project) is complete . . . and the form will appear as it is in Figure 3-2.

8. Next locate the lowest PERT number on the form. Cross it out. Write "1" in the "CHRONOLOCIAL NUMBER" column. Locate the next lowest PERT number, and write "2" in the Chronological Number column. Continue until all tasks are numbered. Now the form appears as in Figure 3-3.

9. Give the form to a clerk. Ask him or her to type a formal procedure. Then the procedure or project will appear as in Figure 3-4. It's ready for action and follow up . . . and progress.

NOTE: The procedure is not complete. Nine steps have been used merely to illustrate how to write a procedure using Poor Man's PERT. Actually, many more steps may be needed. As you continue to work on your PERT, it will get better.

Poor Man's PERT really is that simple. What isn't simple is that it is hard to believe an approach can be effective when it is so simple. The trick is to activate . . . to do a Poor Man's PERT.

3.3 ACTIVATE AND ENJOY SUCCESS WITH POOR MAN'S PERT

Use Poor Man's PERT and write two or three procedures, Mr. Administrator. Perhaps an Instructor Development Program for next year. Then "graduate" into using Poor Man's PERT to plan two or three major projects. Perhaps a different faculty loading system other than credit hours. Perhaps the development of a decision-matrix showing where, by whom and how all decisions are made in your college.

As the administrator progresses in his use of Poor Man's PERT, he sees an excellent opportunity for leadership and for extra progress . . . progress above and beyond that accruing from his own PERTs. So he talks to his subordinates, and he shows them what he did. And he tells of results accomplished and to be accomplished. He motivates them to learn and activate PERT. They do. They progress. He progresses. The college progresses.

OBJECTIVE OR PROCEDURE: To develop a public relations plan in written form for the approval of the Administrative Cabinet by July 1, 20XX			
PERT NO.	CHRON NO.	WHO	WHAT
100		PR Director	Develop PR effort with the news media
50		PR Director	Budget for goals and objectives of PR functions
10		President/Others	Develop goals and objectives to guide PR function
200		PR Director	Develop program of dissemination of official information
15		President	Assign responsibility for coordinating and administering PR function
300		PR Director/Others	Identify the publics it is found necessary to reach
250		PR Director	Develop a plan of evaluation of PR
25		PR Director	Publish PR policies and procedures manual
24		PR Director/President	Decide what is to be included in the PR manual

Figure 3-2. Poor Man's PERT

PERT NO.	CHRON. NO.	WHO	WHAT
	OBJECTIVE OR PROCEDURE: To develop a public relations plan in written form for the approval of the Administrative Cabinet by July 1, 20XX

PERT NO.	CHRON. NO.	WHO	WHAT
~~100~~	6	PR Director	Develop PR effort with the news media
~~50~~	5	PR Director	Budget for goals and objectives of PR functions
~~10~~	1	President/Others	Develop goals and objectives to guide PR function
~~200~~	7	PR Director	Develop program of dissemination of official information
~~15~~	2	President	Assign responsibility for coordinating and administering PR function
~~300~~	9	PR Director/Others	Identify the publics it is found necessary to reach
~~250~~	8	PR Director	Develop a plan of evaluation of PR
~~25~~	4	PR Director	Publish PR policies and procedures manual
~~24~~	3	PR Director/President	Decide what is to be included in the PR manual

Figure 3-3. Poor Man's PERT

OBJECTIVE:	To develop a public relations plan in written form for the approval of the Administrative Cabinet by July 1, 20XX

WHO	WHAT
President/Others	1. Develop goals and objectives to guide PR function
President	2. Assign responsibility for coordinating and administering PR function
PR Director/President	3. Decide what is to be included in PR manual
PR Director	4. Publish PR policies and procedure manual
PR Director	5. Budget for goals and objectives of PR function
PR Director	6. Develop PR effort with the news media
PR Director	7. Develop a program of dissemination of official information
President/PR Director	8. Develop a plan of evaluation of PR
PR Director/Others	9. Identify the publics it is found necessary to reach

Figure 3-4. Completed Procedure from Poor Man's PERT

Then he talks to his peers and superiors. He shows them the results gained from Poor Man's PERT by himself and his subordinates. He prevails on them to do what he did. Some won't. But some will. And those who do will progress. And the college progresses more and more.

3.4 THE ACHIEVING ACTION

Mr. Administrator, Poor Man's PERT is creativity for progress, and look at the pluses it has going for it.

- It shows college progress.
- It helps the administrator increase his own progress.
- It is downright fun. Time flies for the individual who PERTs procedures and projects.
- It gives the image and posture of leadership to the individual who first introduces Poor Man's PERT to his college.

Begin today. Identify a problem then use the Poor Man's PERT form to write down that first task. When that much is done, it will be actually difficult not to follow by writing the next task . . . and the next . . . and the next.
Thus Poor Man's PERT makes progress infectious. Well, if you must have a disease, Mr. Administrator, you can't find a better one than progress-itis.

SUCCESS EXERCISES

After having studied Chapter 3 you should be able to:

(1) Write plans and procedures to the extent that they will be properly established, maintained and implemented
(2) Write plans and procedures such that no task shall be overlooked
(3) Write plans and procedures such that you have control . . . and can spot and solve problems in early stages

3-1   Try a Poor Man's PERT for an objective, plan or procedure of your own choosing. (1) On a copy of Figure 3-1, write in an objective, plan or procedure as it relates to your college or job functions. (2) Now complete by yourself the sequence of WHAT, WHO, PERT NO. and CHRONOLOGICAL NO. (3) Have your administrative assistant retype into correct chronological order.

3-2   Now comes one of the most important uses of Poor Man's PERT. An objective, plan or procedure developed in isolation of your own desk seldom has the support of those who will implement it . . . your subordinates or staff members. The ultimate use of this technique is to develop within a meeting of your staff or subordinates the WHAT, WHO, PERT NO. and CHRONOLOGICAL NO. of a specific objective, plan or procedure. Thus, you will have been synergistic. . . the whole being greater than the sum of the parts. Remember, involvement of others greatly increases their support of that which is developed . . . especially if it affects them either directly or indirectly.

3-3 Use the objective, plan or procedure from exercise 3-1 or establish a completely new one.

3-4 Call a staff meeting where you provide only the objective, plan or procedure to be developed and the headings: PERT NO., CHRON. NO., WHO, and WHAT on the chalkboard or chart pad. Enlist the experience of the people in the meeting in developing the Poor Man's PERT. Be synergistic.

3-5 Reflect on the following questions as they relate to exercise 3-1 and 3-2.

1. If you used the same objective, plan or procedure for both exercises, how do the Poor Man's PERTs compare?
2. If you used a new objective, plan or procedure for exercise 3-2, how well did the group contribute?
3. How successful were you in using this technique for the first time in a meeting?

ACTION POINT: The next time in a meeting where the development of an objective, plan or procedure seems to "bog" down, take charge and sketch on the board or chart pad the four elements: PERT NO., CHRON. NO., WHO, and WHAT. Do your Poor Man's PERT routine and become a hero!

3-6 Place the typed figures of these exercises into your ring binder. Review often for their content. Update each Poor Man's PERT as it becomes necessary to stay relevant.

3-7 Have the people who report to you complete these exercises. Soon your whole college will be experts in developing PLANS and PROCEDURES.

Chapter 4

Make Ideas Make Progress

"Learn Soppada . . . Activate Soppada . . . Spread Soppada"

INTRODUCTION: Whatever your level, Mr. Administrator. . . you can convert your ideas, and the ideas of your associates, into extra progress for your college and more recognition for yourself. The cost-progress squeeze, which is partly a squeeze because more administrators complain about it rather than fight it (and there is plenty of room to win that fight), is not about to close out the progress for the college which promotes activating the ideas of its people.

The name of this game is "Soppada" . . . and examples of Soppada's dramatic results number in the thousands. One case: A large college tested 33 people. The test included hypothetical, competitive situations . . . a "what would you do now" approach. The purpose of the test was to tab people for close watching, in regard to promotions. An added starter was this: A deanship was open at the time and would be filled by one of the people being tested.

One of the people had learned Soppada. So she used Soppada, in her arriving at and expressing her solutions to the hypothetical situations. Results: (1) She scored high above the others . . . and these were all darned good people. (2) She was told, on the day of the test, that she was promoted to dean.

A college, one of the largest in the southeast, was humming along pretty well. The president of this college, having mastered Soppada himself, thought he'd use the approach in order to cause even more progress. He began weekly half-hour meetings with his key people. The rules of this game: Every key person would bring one Soppada per week. Discussion of these Soppadas took place in the meetings . . . evaluations leading toward ultimate submissions of the Soppadas as proposals for improvement.

Results: (1) In the first year, over 100 Soppada ideas activated. (2) Curiosity of other people was aroused, so that their Soppada meetings have been recently activated. (3) The strong probability is that this is a permanent and continuing thing.

Many administrators are so busy mopping up the floor that they don't have time to turn off the faucet. Most improvements, and there are very few being activated in relation to the opportunities, come forth as reaction to emergencies. Planned improvements center in the traditional areas of instructional development, cost efficiency (usually the improvements here are noodled out by men who do not do the actual work . . . no Edisons, these), data processing (converting manual tasks to machines), and so on.

Not that these traditional improvement areas are wrong directions. Far from it. They are very right directions, and continuous assiduous attention to these areas may well be the difference between a great college and an average one. The fact is that attacking traditional improvement areas is not enough. Imagination is a wandering bee and is quite likely to settle on flowers we don't even know are in the progress meadow.

To maximize progress through improvements . . . to give competition fits and trustees that warm and cozy feeling. . . administrators must take three giant steps forward. They must:

1. Learn Soppada
2. Activate Soppada
3. Spread Soppada

4.1 LEARN SOPPADA

S   ubject

O   bjective

P   resent Situation

P   roposal

A   dvantages

D   isadvantages

A   ction

That's Soppada: The seven elements of progress reasoning. Easy to understand. Not too difficult to write a Soppada . . . and not too easy, either. It's deceptive in its simple appearance. Application of a Soppada, as with application of new thinking anywhere, is somewhat difficult. However, Soppada is no more difficult to create and activate than is any other method of reasoning. . . and Soppada works better.

For a frame of reference, let's use Soppada as a way to write a progressive idea. The idea is in the mind of Ila Seymore. Ila is office manager of the college typing pool, and she is bugged because paperwork is getting heavier and heavier. She sees her college fighting increasing correspondence by adding more junior administrators. And with each junior administrator seems to come a typist. Then both of them become more expensive. The junior administrator becomes a senior administrator (in title, anyway). The typist, by some magic of communications that administrators have never figured out, becomes a "secretary." Not really a secretary (there are very few secretaries on the college scene . . . lots of typists) . . . but a secretary in title. And anyone knows that secretaries get more money than typists . . . and that senior administrators get more money than junior administrators.

So Ila has an idea that her college, by judicious use of precedent letters, can get out more letters of higher quality more quickly and at less cost. She feels, and quite properly so, that if college letters are superior to competitors' letters, she will have something of an edge on her competitors . . . with the resultant extra progress. On the other hand, Ila knows that activating her idea will trigger insecurity explosions from the junior/senior administrators and typists/secretaries who are now making a living off the present cumbersome, costly and ineffective approaches. And she knows that her idea, being a change, will incur progressive challenges.

A good idea. But the good idea comprises a mishmash of reasoning and good points and bad points and chips of logic which if presented, would torpedo the idea by the very weight of its oral complexity. And that's where Soppada comes in. It separates the man-points from the boy-points. It enables Ila to present, simply and quickly and clearly and objectively, her idea. It enables Ila to present her idea so well that, assuming the idea has merit (Soppada will not phony up and sell a bad idea), it will be accepted by her boss. Here, then, is Ila's Soppada:

SUBJECT: Guide Letters

OBJECTIVE: That all college letters shall be based on top-quality precedent, consistent with college policy.

PRESENT SITUATION: Letters are dictated cold. Quality varies in accordance with personal skills and pressure of other work at the time of dictation. This quality is not an acceptable standard.

PROPOSAL: Extra copies of all dictated letters be kept, reviewed, improved, indexed, bound and used as future guides. Specifically:

1. File extra copies of all dictated correspondence
2. Review the file weekly
3. Improve the letters
4. Index the improved letters
5. Obtain management approval for using the letters as guides (A guide letter is not usually used word for word . . . it is used as the basis for letters covering similar recurring situations.)
6. Place the approved letters in a guide letter binder . . . for continuing use as precedent letters

ADVANTAGES:

1. Letters will be "predictable." All will be as approved by management.
2. Top-quality letters are assured. After all, these letters are our college's most powerful Direct-Mail Advertising Campaign.
3. Actual preparation of letters can be done on lower levels, merely on the basis of symbols furnished by administrators.

DISADVANTGES:

1. Habit. Initially, it will be hard to break the habit of cold dictation. However, once formed, the new habit will be stronger than the old habit.
2. Ego. Initially, administrators will think their thoughts are being regimented. However, ultimate good results will make for an even stronger ego.

ACTION:

Next Monday, please instruct all typists to file extra copies of dictated correspondence, referring the copies to me on the following Friday. This should continue until further notice.

Why does Soppada work? What makes it better than any other method of presenting ideas? Well Soppada puts Ila's thoughts into a creatively chronological order. It doesn't make her smarter. It does, however, bring her full intelligence into use and into light. Here's how:

The first element of progress reasoning (**Subject**) can be compared to the label on a bottle of pills. The label tells what is in the bottle. So it is that the **Subject**, the label of the Soppada, tells what is in the proposal. Referring back to Ila's Soppada, it is seen that the label is "Guide Letters." But writing the Subject logs one more important plus for Ila: The conscious act of writing the Subject has temporarily "narrowed" Ila's mind to concentrate on the creative aspects of that Subject. She has marshaled the forces of her conscious and unconscious and her subconscious minds (and whatever other kinds the scientific people say there are).

The **Objective** is, of course, the goal . . . the end result to be attained. The act of writing the **Objective** triggers a motivation to attain it. Put it this way: When Ila writes her **Objective**, she places a carrot ahead of her own nose. This is a much more acceptable challenge than when someone else puts the challenge there.

Writing the **Present Situation** further motivates Ila. Ila is unhappy with the Present Situation. That was the "healthy discontent" that motivated her to attack the problem in the first place. Having now written the **Objective** (where she wants to be) and the **Present Situation** (where she is now), Ila is highly motivated to make the trip from "where she is" to "where she wants to be."

The word "Problem" is not included in the Soppada. But Soppada does define the problem. Because the problems of colleges are all the same and always the same. The problem of an administrator is always to get from where he is (the **Present Situation**) to where he wants to be (the **Objective**). By writing the **Objective** and the **Present Situation**, the administrator has stated the problem. Defining a problem, per se, is never necessary, in spite of the presentations to the contrary from "scientific" analysts who have spent much of their lives promoting problem-solving. Forget problem-solving. Use Soppada.

The interesting thing about the **Proposal**, the fourth element of progress-reasoning, is that its steps will, at this point, come almost naturally to Ila . . . even though she was not aware of these steps when she began her Soppada. Here's why:

Ila's mind is now in a chronologically creative process. By temporarily narrowing her mind to concentrate on the matter at hand (writing the Subject) and by motivating herself by writing her **Objective** and her **Present Situation** . . . Ila has used her own wonderful mental powers, as her mind releases and her hand writes the basic (not necessarily detailed) steps that will get her from the **Present Situation** to the **Objective**.

Ila will be sold on Soppada at this point. In fact, she'll think she has a complete idea, and she'll be sorely tempted to march it in, in its present form, to her superior. She must resist that temptation. Impulsiveness may be attractive, in that it is often mistaken for enthusiasm . . . but impulsiveness does not pave the administrator's progress roadway.

So Ila must now write the fifth element of progress-reasoning: the **Advantages**. Advantages are the benefits which the college will gain when (not if) the idea is sold and accepted. Another temptation must be resisted here . . . the temptation to write too many **Advantages**, to "oversell." The three (never more) main Advantages should be written. If there are more, and there probably are, they should be saved for oral rebuttal, when the superior questions the proposer. Left-over **Advantages** are Sunday Punches . . . and can, when brought in orally, make the difference between acceptance and rejection of an idea.

As easy and pleasant as it is to identify and write **Advantages**, it is even more difficult to change pace and write the sixth element of progress-reasoning: the **Disadvantages**. By the time Ila has completed her **Advantages**, she is ready to swear that there just plain aren't any **Disadvantages**. She means it, too. Her emotional level is so high that she may truly be unable to find a Disadvantage. But she must. Because **Disadvantages** are there. And if they are not listed . . . and if Ila's superior finds them . . . the superior will suspect an "unbalanced presentation." The idea may die right there, because it was rigged "for acceptance only."

So Ila must throttle back on her emotions. She should use this guide: There are always two **Disadvantages** to any idea . . . (1) It involves a change, therefore it will incur resentment, and (2) It will cost something.

Two disadvantages should be written, and these must be honest portrayals of the two major **Disadvantages**. Each **Disadvantage** must come in two sentences. The first sentence describes the **Disadvantage**. The second sentence begins with the word "however" . . . followed by a description of how that **Disadvantage** will ultimately be overcome. Written forthrightly, a **Disadvantage** actually becomes an **Advantage**.

And still the idea is not ready for presentation. Seems to be, but it isn't. Ila, you see, is human . . . and therefore imperfect. Being imperfect, Ila is not completely predictable. Being unpredictable, Ila is likely to pull a crazy stunt or two in order to activate her idea. It is this boat rocking threat that causes many superiors to "hold" ideas, neither accepting or rejecting, until they disappear into some clerical Never-Never Land that is the constant frustration of your administrators who have been heard to mutter, "That old XXX in the ivory tower never buys anything. I'll bet the first idea of mine he'll ever buy will be my resignation."

So Ila writes her seventh element of progress-reasoning: **Action**. Here she describes, in detail, the first step she'll take when (not if) her idea is accepted. **Action** makes her predictable. It tells exactly what she is going to do. The **Action** statement on a Soppada has saved many a progressive idea from Never-Never Land.

4.2 ACTIVATE SOPPADA

No matter how well it is prepared and presented, rarely if ever will an idea be accepted, word for word, as it was presented. Ila's superior, for dead certain, is going to make a number of editing comments. At first, Ila will resent this tampering. Makes her feel the same way she did when she dented the fender on her car the same day she bought it . . . ill.

But most top-level administrators are where they are for good reason. Ila's boss is Ila's boss because he is a pretty smart guy running a pretty solid department. The boss's editions will, on objective reflection, probably make sense. So Ila compromises. She rewrites her Soppada.

Maybe she rewrites it several times. And maybe it is this attention to final competence (as opposed to going in to a monumental sulk because the boss is "unreasonable") that separates the men from the boys in this exciting but difficult business of getting an idea into operation.

In time, an idea will be accepted. Maybe not the first Soppada. Maybe not the fourth or fifth. But an idea will be accepted. And, the idea successfully implemented. Following one acceptance, Ila will be motivated toward more and more and more. The creative monkey is on her back. Which is a nice way to be hooked. That monkey isn't heavy at all.

Ila activates her Soppada, because acceptance doesn't make her Soppada complete. Only successful activation makes it complete. So Ila mother-hens her Soppada through its installation, and to the point where habits have changed, where people's complaints are back to their normal level, and to the point where the college is making more progress because of the idea. And then (not on acceptance) is when Ila should expect her quid pro quo. Despite the cries of men who think much and act little (I'll give them an idea when they give me enough money to make it worth my while), rewards for progressive ideas do come forth . . . after they work.

Makes sense. You can't warm your hands by the stove until first you put in a little wood to burn.

4.3 SPREAD SOPPADA

Now Ila has activated several Soppadas. She's hooked on progress-reasoning. She earns more money now. She's on the move. And she discovers, as all administrators ultimately do, that the simple fact of college life is this: She is not paid for working hard, for being lovable, for going to night school, or even for having ideas. She is paid for results . . . for the results that come forth from her area of responsibility.

Recognizing why she is valuable, Ila creates Seymore's Law, which states: "It is good for a man to work hard and competently . . . to add his brains and muscles to the organization . . . to be of maximum effectiveness; however, a man not only adds himself to his organization . .

. he multiplies himself within it." A man multiplies himself within his organization by teaching others to be as good (preferably better, if he is a leader) as he is.

Thus Ila, from the strong base of her own success, teaches Soppada to others. She wheedles, she cajoles, she persuades, she motivates. Some (not all, ever . . . but some) follow. Some learn and activate Soppada. One day Ila's area of the college stands out so clearly from other areas, in its attitudes and in its progress contributions, that Ila is inevitably called to higher and better positions and fatter pay checks.

4.4 THE ACHIEVING ACTION

Mr. Administrator, begin writing a Soppada now . . . right this minute, on a form similar to Figure 4-1. If you write only the Subject and the Objective, begin now . . . right this minute. If you do, you'll be motivated to finish the job you start now . . . right this minute. And if you finish one Soppada, you'll be hooked on progressive creativity.

You may wind up with a whole book full of Soppadas. Aside from their value to the college . . . think of what a great book that one would be when read by a sharp young person you hired in . . . or a comer whom you oriented. Let's face it. Wouldn't that practical book of Soppadas be better reading than a "wise" treatise composed from reference material by a professor in a university library?

Mr. Administrator, make a follow-up note. Six months from today, ask yourself: "How many Soppadas have I completed? How many are activated? How many other people have learned Soppada from me? What are their results?" Satisfy yourself with your answers to these questions . . . and you can bet you're satisfying your top people and are meeting or exceeding the goals of your college.

SUCCESS EXERCISES

After having studied Chapter 4 you should be able to:

(1) Develop your ideas in a precise written form
(2) Sell (implement) you ideas

4-1   Now it is time for you to write a Soppada with your own Subject and Objective. You may wish to return to Chapter 2 and select an Objective from which to construct a Soppada; otherwise develop one to your liking. On a copy of Figure 4-1 complete your Soppada.

4-2   Having completed exercise 4-1, you are now ready to sell your idea. Go to the person to whom you report. Present your Soppada . . . Expect to have some discussion and maybe even modification. Get his approval to implement your idea.

4-3   Place your completed Soppadas in your ring binder. Implement the ones that were good enough for you to sell. Examine those that you could not sell. If the objective is still of priority . . . rewrite into a better Soppada and then try selling again.

4-4   Have the people who report to you complete these exercises. Soon everyone will be using Soppada . . . and will they ever Learn, Activate, and Spread Soppada!

SUBJECT:
OBJECTIVE:
PRESENT SITUATION:
PROPOSAL: 1. 2. 3. 4.
ADVANTAGES: 1. 2. 3.
DISADVANTAGES: 1. 2.
ACTION:

Figure 4-1. SOPPADA: A Progress-Causing Idea

4-5 Review Chapters 1-3. Write a Soppada to implement in your organization the specific ideas of each chapter. Continue the practice of writing a Soppada after each chapter that you read in this book (and other books).

Chapter 5

More Meetings, More Progress

"Standardize the meeting's objective . . . End the meeting on time . . . Maximize standup meetings"

INTRODUCTION: On the surface, it would seem to bespeak courage or stupidity . . . to tell colleges to hold more meetings. Most administrators say they have too many meetings already. Some have even been tempted to outlaw meetings entirely, so as to "get a little work done."

And small wonder that administrators feel this way. They have, for years, witnessed the wheel-spinning of meetings which dragged on for hours, only to end because the day ended . . . and where the conferees were no closer to solutions than when these meetings began. And they have been on the receiving end of complaints by parents that phone calls to Mrs. X . . . trying to get information about their son or daughter being admitted to the college . . . always seemed to be answered by the comment, "He is in a meeting."

In spite of these very real minuses, it is not stupid to promote more meetings. Nor does one need courage to take this hard stand in favor of more meetings. All that is needed is logic. Because the case in favor of more meetings is based on intelligent reasoning.

If your college is graduating two thousand students a year. . . and if two thousand students is all your business community or senior college can absorb . . . and if, in the past forty years of doing college business, two thousand students per year is all your college ever did graduate . . . and if there is no need for new programs or future possibility of ever graduating more than two thousand students . . . and each year you have more money to spend that you possibly can . . . then there is very little need for meetings.

You would know exactly what to do next year, and the next year, and the next. You would need no new people to recruit students, look for money, or develop new programs or employment opportunities for graduates. You'd need maintenance men, deans, vice presidents and a president . . . but these people would be solidly set in their jobs which never did or never would change. These people would never need a meeting.

But most colleges are directly opposite of the status quo. Even the most conservative record that a good percent of the curriculum programs offered today were not offered twenty years ago . . . and some as recent as five years ago in electronics. And next year, more programs will have to be placed on the drawing board for consideration for your own dynamic progress and requirements to keep up with the times and Tofler's "Future Shocked" world.

Now you can write memos and design forms. And you should. Both have their places. Both communicate well. But in the quickening climate of America's ingenuity, only the meeting stands out as the single best form of communications. It is the only form of communication which gives administrators two important pluses at the same time: eyeball-to-eyeball contact and the opportunity for rebuttal.

Administrators never did have too many meetings. They merely had too many ineffective meetings. And they spent too many hours in those ineffective meetings. This being so, then the solution is not to eliminate or reduce the number of meetings.

The solution is to make meetings make more progress. And they will, to the extent that we solve the great mystery of meetings: "Why is so much time and energy wasted on a communications medium (meetings) which, when done properly, has the biggest progress potential of them all?"

The answer is simple. It does not lie in the books on behavioral science or in the beautifully-worded "new" concepts about which much business education centers. Oh, sure . . . the books and the courses give good answers. But not good enough. If the books and the speeches were all that good, then there wouldn't be ineffective meetings.

Effective and progress-causing meetings will benefit the administrator who sees to it that three rules are followed. These rules are:

1. Standardize the meeting's objective
2. End the meeting on time
3. Maximize stand-up meetings

5.1 STANDARDIZE THE MEETING'S OBJECTIVE

For the next meeting coming up, and for every meeting thereafter, be sure that the first item of the meeting is the objective. Agreement (and if not agreement, at least understanding) of all conferees, on the objective of the meeting, must be taken care of before any further discussion takes place. The objective must be written, on their note pads, by all conferees . . . and each objective must be written word-for-word alike. The alternative may be hours of unfinished sentences, false starts, short tempers and no end results.

The objective of a meeting, by the way, is never to discuss anything. Discussion is done, of course. But discussion is the method of attaining the objective . . . it is never the objective itself. The objective of a meeting is an expression of what must happen as a result of the meeting. And if the result doesn't happen in the meeting, but will take place later, then the meeting leader is responsible (or will assign the responsibility) for following up until the objective is attained.

The objective of a meeting should be clearly and simply worded. Here are a few examples which will serve as patterns for objectives:

1. To obtain approval of, and activate, the proposed new Weekly Status Report (to follow in Chapter 7)
2. To establish a student recruitment plan for the new diesel mechanics program
3. To decide if we should develop a new microelectronics program . . . if so, to complete the development of that program by "Z" date
4. To approve, adjust or reject the proposed college budget for next year's operations

Once the wording of an objective is agreed on, meetings will move fast and will get results. Always begin meetings by establishing written objectives.

5.2 END THE MEETING ON TIME

As soon as the objective is established, the meeting leader should announce the time the meeting will end.

Administrators rarely announce ending times . . . yet, this is of vital importance if the meeting is to include full cooperation and concentration. When a conferee knows that the meeting will be over at 9:45 a.m., his mind is free to do the meeting's work.

When a conferee does not know the meeting's ending time, he will quite likely fret. His mind will stray. These are some of the questions which will nag at his mind and will pull his concentration away from the objective at hand:

1. The computer engineer is coming in at 10:30. How can I get out of this meeting and get going on that automated student registration program?
2. I told John Stokes I'd meet him at the Country Club for lunch. Now, I wonder if this meeting will make me late . . . or if I'll get there at all.
3. I promised the XYZ Company I'd phone reference the five graduates they phoned about. If I don't follow up and then get to phone them, I'm going to have an unhappy camper.

But if the conferee knows when the meeting will end, then he knows he'll have time for his other "musts" . . . and there are plenty of "musts" these days. His mind won't dwell outside the meeting. He'll be sharp and effective.

Administrators, in spite of the fact that many of them say this can't be done, do know when meetings will end . . . and for the most part their instincts and experience bring them pretty close. And, in the case where a meeting must run over (and this will happen), do this: End the meeting on time anyway . . . and call another short meeting for the next day.

The advantage is this: In the nearly 24 hours between meetings, the mind of each conferee will be, consciously or subconsciously, working on the problem. Conferees will arrive at the second meeting ready and able to conclude much more quickly than if meeting number one was allowed to run on and on. Which means this: Two meetings totaling two hours time and twice as many meetings as one meeting going all day. But (and this is the progress angle) twice as many meetings will have taken one-fourth the total time!

End all meetings at or before an announced time. It saves time and valuable energy . . . and gives better results.

5.3 MAXIMIZE STAND-UP MEETINGS

There are certain meetings which must be lengthy. Not many, but some. For these meetings, it is right and proper to provide, for the conferees, as much comfort as possible. Chairs, tables, ashtrays, note pads, pencils, and so on.

But the vast majority of meetings need not be lengthy. Some, in fact, can be wrapped up in a surprisingly short time. So, the purpose of the stand-up meeting is not to make people uncomfortable. Its purpose is to eliminate "burrowing-in."

When people come to meetings, some do "burrow in." They get comfortable. They prepare for pipe-smoking, pipe-cleaning, coffee-drinking, and so on. Mentally, they get ready for a long session. You know, a stand-up meeting can be held and adjourned in the time it takes just to get up a head of steam for an as-usual meeting. Something like a cold shower: It gets the job done, one doesn't linger, and it feels good afterward. Here are the four simple steps to the payoffs to be gained from stand-up meetings:

First, stand-up yourself. As conferees arrive, ask them not to be seated . . . "because this will be a short session."

Standing conferees are not resentful when the meeting leader is also standing.

Second, distribute clip boards to key people. When you invite them to sit-down meetings, make no mention of the clip boards. But when you call a stand-up meeting, tell them: "Bring your clip boards, please. You may want to take a few notes." By the time you have called your second stand-up meeting (the first one is, admittedly, a bit of a shock), conferees will understand that "bring your clip board" means "we stand at this one."

Third (as covered before in this chapter), standardize the meeting's objective. No matter how demanding the panic, save time by taking time for all conferees to understand the objective. For example, you may announce it this way: "Ladies and Gentlemen, the Board of Regents phoned about our projected enrollment for next year. I promised to phone back within the hour. So, the purpose of this session is to determine projected enrollments within your respective divisions and arrive at a college total."

Fourth, hold the meeting. Decide on the problems and hurdles to be overcome . . . and arrive at a firm conclusion so that the promised phone call can be made, on time, to the Board of Regents.

Now, all colleges are different. Individual college differences do stand out. This is one of the features which makes college management exciting. Therefore, the words of this chapter must be shaped and adjusted to exactly fit each college.

But all colleges are alike in one respect. If they do not try a new idea, they will certainly never benefit from it. Try it. Try more meetings for more progress. And, as administrators know they must, keep score. Here is a short series of questions. Put them in a follow-up file for three months. Then pull them out. See if you met your own high standards for achievement:

1. What percentage of your meetings begin with an agreed-on (or understood) objective? Were these meetings more effective because the objectives were set?
2. What percentage of your meetings are ending on time? Have you found that just as much or more gets done, even though arbitrary ending times are being set?
3. What percentage of your meetings are stand-up meetings? Have you been able to spread this concept through your entire college? Are you satisfied with results to date?

When the answers to these questions bespeak progress, don't give credit to the authors. Credit yourself. Anybody can give advice . . . but it takes a big person to shape that advice, make it work, and keep it working. My congratulations to you... in advance.

SUCCESS EXERCISES

After having studied Chapter 5 you should be able to:

(1) Get more results from fewer meetings
(2) Follow up meeting commitments to ensure results

5-1 Using a copy of Figure 5-1 as a guide (1) Call a slow meeting (a slow meeting is one that is called 24 hours in advance). Be sure that the WHAT and WHEN meet all the requirements of this chapter. (2) Make an effort to ensure that the WHAT of the meeting will require follow-up and commitment of those who attended. (3) Have someone keep the meeting commitments on a copy of Figure 5-2. (4) After the meeting have the "meeting commitments" typed and distributed to the persons who attended.

5-2 After having held the meeting of Exercise 5-1, mentally reflect on how you could have made the meeting a better one. List below the specific things you will do differently for the next slow meeting:

a. _____

b. _____

c. _____

d. _____

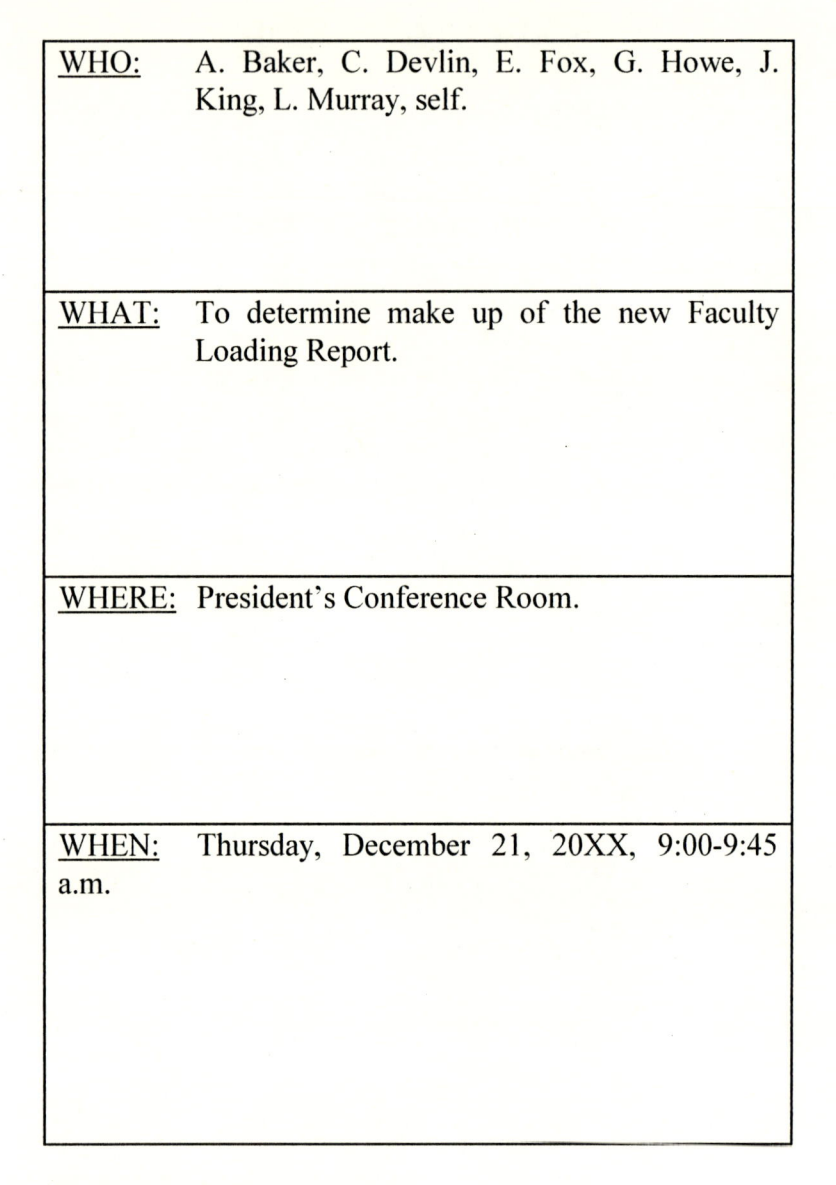

<u>WHO:</u>	A. Baker, C. Devlin, E. Fox, G. Howe, J. King, L. Murray, self.
<u>WHAT:</u>	To determine make up of the new Faculty Loading Report.
<u>WHERE:</u>	President's Conference Room.
<u>WHEN:</u>	Thursday, December 21, 20XX, 9:00-9:45 a.m.

Figure 5-1. A Slow Meeting

WHO	WHAT	WHEN

Figure 5-2. Meeting Commitments

5-3 A "quick meeting" is an emergency-type meeting. It is called with little notice. Between the time you call the meeting and time the people arrive in your office, write down the WHAT of the meeting. Using a copy of Figure 5-3, accomplish the following activities:

   a. Decide on a WHAT for the meeting
   b. Call the people who can help you with the WHAT... ask them to rush right over
   c. As soon as they arrive, have each person write the WHAT down on a piece of paper (don't be surprised if you have to furnish the paper!)
   d. Accomplish the objective of the meeting

5-4 This exercise is intended to introduce you to the "quick stand-up" meeting. It may be necessary to remove all the chairs from your office or conference room to be successful! Decide on the WHAT for the meeting. After having the WHAT written similar to Figure 5-3, then do the following:

   a. Call an individual to your office and ask him to bring a paper pad to write on (or clipboard). After this meeting, asking the individual to bring a clipboard will serve as a signal of the "quick stand-up" meeting.
   b. When he arrives tell him the WHAT and have him write it down (with no chairs he will have to stand!). You should always stand yourself when conducting a stand-up meeting. Expect your first "quick stand-up" meeting not to work. However, the first one will allow you to establish the rules, signals, and procedures of having a "quick stand-up" meeting with your people.

| WHAT: | To furnish the Board of Trustees' chairperson with information on the status of House Bill 1389 |

Figure 5-3. A Quick Meeting

Chapter 6

Time Management

"When the administrator analyzes, in detail, everything he does on the job . . . the result is sharply increased productivity."

INTRODUCTION: Stancey Unnorris, President, Unnorris College was frustrated. "I work hard. My people work hard. Still, I have the feeling that I should be more effective. And I have the feeling that my people should be getting more results out of all the work they do. But I simply don't know how to shoehorn more work into my own schedule . . . or into my people's schedules."

Well, Dr. Unnorris . . . we can say here that what you're talking about is "productivity." And your frustration is shared by a lot of college people who are busy and are successful but who still have the same feeling that they could get more results from a work week.

There's a simple reason why this feeling persists. The reason is: It's logical. It's right. People can be more productive. And I'd like to propose to you . . . exactly how I feel you . . . and anyone in your college . . . can be more productive.

"All right. Let's have it."

Four steps. Here they are:

1. Write one week's action
2. Recap the week's action
3. Analyze the week's action
4. Get the payoff

6.1 WRITE ONE WEEK'S ACTION

There can be no glossing over the flat fact that I am proposing for you to spend what may very well be your most unpleasant week ever.

"Doesn't sound very appetizing. Frankly, it sounds like a proposal I'm going to turn down."

Don't turn it down yet, Dr. Unnorris. Let me give you razor-sharp reasons to consider going through this traumatic week.

"Go ahead. Propose away. But it sounds pretty bad to me."

Okay. Reason number one: The result of your worst week ever will be increased productivity for you. The result will show on your bottom line.

"I like that bottom-line part. You have another reason?"

Sure do, Dr. Unnorris. Look . . . you're President of Unnorris College.

"Darned right I am. And the only President Unnorris College has ever had."

I'm aware of that, sir. The point I want to make is this: As President, you are an example. When you put yourself through a program of time control, then your subordinates will find it hard to not do the same, when you ask them.

"If I tell them to do whatever this is, they had darned well better do it."

I don't recommend administrative clout here, Dr. Unnorris. A little bit of pressure, sure . . . but not too much. If people don't want to spend this horrible week, forcing them would not bring progress results.

"But I sure can make note of who does and who doesn't for future pay raises and promotions."

That you can, Dr. Unnorris. And I propose you do exactly that. The individual who accepts the program should be favored over the person who does not. And that brings me to my reason number two: The result of the program, with each of your people, will be increased productivity . . . and each result will show on your bottom line.

Now . . . here's why the week to be is horrible. Because, from the beginning of work day one through the end of work on day five . . . I ask you to write down what you did with every single minute of your time.

"Wow! That is a bad week."

It sure is, Dr. Unnorris. But I can relieve your mind a little. Consider these points:

> 1. When you perform a task, give that task a number. From that point, every time you perform that same task . . . merely use the number. That'll save some time.
>
> Take a look at Figure 6-1. It shows the way your record is going to appear. You'll notice that, from 8:30 a.m. through 8:46 a.m., the individual listed "1. Opened, read and made notes on incoming mail." So, at other times during the week, when the individual performs that same task, he will merely list his time and the identifying number. For example, when afternoon mail is delivered, he will write "1:15 - 1."

8:30 – 8:46	1.	Opened, read, and made notes on incoming mail
8:47	2.	Answered phone
8:53	3.	Made phone call
9:00	4.	Analyzed Faculty Load Report
10:05	3.	
10:15	5.	Dictated
11:19	6.	Potty
Etc.		

Figure 6-1. Daily "Minutes" Log

2. You are busy. Very busy. But you, as most college people . . . don't do as many different things as you might think. Perhaps, in any given week, you'll do eight or nine different things. So, you'll merely log entries of numbers . . . and won't need to do very much writing of words.

3. You do get interruptions, certainly. On the other hand, you also do get a fair number of long "mental production runs." By that I mean you do get, at times, 30-minute or one-hour periods . . . or even longer stretches . . . when you are working on a single thing. Examples could be:

   A. Dictating letters

   B. Analyzing and making action-to-take notes . . . from monthly financial reports

   C. Conducting a meeting

Where you do have these long mental production runs, your entry time . . . to the Minutes Log . . . will be just a few seconds out of the hour. So it is that the annoyance of maintaining the log is not in the time spent making entries. Indeed, making entries takes very little time . . . perhaps a half hour out of the entire week. The bad thing is keeping the log always at hand . . . carrying the doggoned thing every place you go.

"All right. I buy your proposal. I'll make out the log, beginning Monday."

Why wait until Monday? Today is Wednesday. Start tomorrow, Thursday. All you need is five days. Any five days. Start Thursday and wind up next Wednesday.

"Okay. I'll start tomorrow. And . . . I have a question."

Yes . . .

"What do I write when I go to the bathroom?"

Take another look at Figure 6-1, Dr. Unnorris. It's right there.

"It is at that. It surely is."

6.2 RECAP THE WEEK'S ACTION

Finally, the bad week ends. Forty hours of work are logged, by the minute. From this point, time control becomes pleasant. Even exciting.

The action now is to write a master report . . . a recap . . . of the week's activities. To recap, just (1) Total the number of times you performed a certain task, and (2) Total the hours and minutes given to that task. Figure 6-2 shows the form to use. And it shows a few of the entries on how one person's recap might look.

"I can see the direction of your thinking here. And I'm pleased about that. But one week is never the same as another. Seems to me the recap can't be accurate."

Doesn't need to be accurate, Dr. Unnorris. The data you get from any week will serve to attain the objective of making you more productive. You'll see how that works out in the third course of action, coming up right now.

6-3. ANALYZE THE WEEK'S ACTION

Here's where real excitement begins. Here's where the coming results are going to pop right out at you.

Take a look at Figure 6-3. This form is made out for each of the different tasks performed during Trauma Week. In other words, if you performed ten different tasks, then you'll head up ten separate forms. After that come the analyses . . . and more results than you'd have thought possible.

As you find the time, pick up each of the Task Analysis forms. Against each of the tasks, ask the five questions listed.

The first question is: "Who else can do this?" And if you are doing something . . . and if someone below your level can do that thing . . . then it's your job to get that thing delegated to a lower level. And, of all the things you do . . . you are going to find at least one . . . perhaps more . . . that should be delegated.

Now I know you don't have a platoon of people sitting around waiting for more work. So maybe you won't get that delegating done today or next week or even next month. But make a note about this, on the Task Analysis form. And noodle on the problem. In reasonable time, you'll get the task delegated. Then you'll have time for the more important tasks that do require your own attention.

"Then, as my vice presidents . . . and others down the line. . . activate time control . . . they'll be making room by doing theirown delegating."

Right. That's the way it works.

"But I detect a flaw."

Flaw. What flaw?

"What happens when you get down to the department heads? Seems to me they'll be overworked. They're going to receive delegation from a higher level but have no way to delegate in turn. What's your answer to that?"

DESCRIPTION OF TASK	TIMES PERFORMED	TOTAL HOURS
1. Opened, read, and made notes on incoming mail	10	2 + 40 min.
2. Answered phone	45	4 + 30
3. Made phone call	38	1 + 56
4. Analyzed Faculty Load Report	1	0 + 55
5. Dictated	13	6 + 50
Etc.		
Etc.		
Etc.		

Figure 6-2. Task Recap

Task Description:
Who Else Can Do This?
What is a Better Way to Do This?
Where is a Better Place to Do This?
What is a Better Time to Do This?
Why Do This at All?

Figure 6-3. Task Analysis

Easy. Delegation done from department heads is what you automate. Department heads' low-level work goes on the computer. That's what a computer is for.

"Best explanation I've had for that monster since I brought the darned thing into the college."

Next question is: "What is a better way to do this?" And here you hit a real jackpot. Being busy, most people don't take time to consider better ways to do things. And those better ways do exist on everything we do. And, while we aren't smart enough to come up with all the answers, we certainly are smart enough to get some of them.

When you ask this "better way" question of yourself, you trigger your relevant creativity. By this I mean that your data bank . . . that remarkable brain you and I carry around . . . will provide output. That output will be data relevant to the question.

From my experience, I can tell you that you will come up with ideas . . . better ways to do a full third or all the tasks you performed during Horror Week. So make notes, on the Task Analysis form, of these ideas. Later, you'll go back and engineer those notes into improvements.

"Are you telling me that I'm doing one-third of my job that badly?"

No, sir. Chances are you're doing things quite well. After all, your work habits did result in your now being president of Unnorris College.

"I'm the charter president."

I know that, Dr. Unnorris. But the point I want to make is this: You aren't doing things badly. It's just that those things can be done better. By you. And by all your people. And after you reap that "What is a better way" harvest, we're ready for the next question on the Task Analysis form.

The next question is: "Where is a better place to do this?" And here the answers can be as simple as the better positioning of work on your desk . . . to doing the thing in another place . . . or even merging two separate tasks and doing them at one time in one place.

You'll find that at least one of the things you are doing could be done in another location. And be done more effectively. Might even be that you could better analyze your financial reports on the potty.

"I believe I could, at that. I always take along something to read. And I have a telephone in there, too. Like the President."

You are the president, Dr. Unnorris.

"No, I mean 'the' President."

Oh! "That" President.

So. Now. Next: "When is a better time to do this?" In this analysis, you are going to find at least one thing, perhaps more... where timing can be improved. Here are some possible examples:

1. Let's say that, in your week, you made 38 telephone calls. Chances are you made them at sporadic times during your days, as conditions suggested the calls.

    Could be, though, that you could make notes and save those calls. Make the calls in mental production runs twice a day. Likely this wouldn't hurt your public image . . . and you do "get hot" when you concentrate single tasks into mental production runs. In other words, your phone calls would be more effective this way.

2. And let's say that you opened incoming mail ten times a week. Who says you must interrupt

your work flow and dig into mail the instant it hits your desk?

But that's what most people do. Seems to me most people are at the mercy of the mail clerk.

Let the mail wait. Open it once a day. Discipline yourself to long mental production runs.

. . . and you'll find other examples, as you analyze your own work habits.

"I know you're right. But an unopened envelope excites me. I'm curious. I've got to see what's in there."
Fight it.
"Okay."
The next question is: "Why do this at all?" And here may come your biggest surprise. Nearly always . . . a solid 90% of the time. . . people who go through this time-control analysis find they are doing something which doesn't need to be done at all.

Could be you're performing some task which was, at one time, quite necessary. But changing conditions may now render that task not useful at all. Or, indeed . . . some task being performed may turn out to be merely a bad habit in need of correction.

Whatever this useless task is, asking "Why do this at all?" will bring that task to consciousness, for objective inspection. You'll probably find such a task. And eliminate it. And thus make more time for the more important tasks that deserve your attention.

"Darned if I can think of anything like that. I don't think I'm doing anything that shouldn't be done."

84

Perhaps not, Dr. Unnorris. But the odds are against you. Chances are that no-should-do task is in there somewhere. I ask that you search for it.

"Okay. I'll look for it."

6.4 GET THE PAYOFF

Now, let's review, Dr. Unnorris. At this point, you will have (1) Completed your One-Week "Minutes" Log, (2) Recapped the week's action, (3) Analyzed every task you performed. Now comes activation.

Your basis for activation are the Task Analysis forms. You have several . . . 8 or 9 or 10 or so. Each form has your notes, notes of actions you will take to improve your productivity. Now take these six steps:

1. Obtain a pad.
2. On your pad, write your action notes, transferring them from your Task Analysis forms.
3. On the job, activate action notes. Consider each a project.
4. When a project is completed, cross it out.
5. Work the projects until all are completed.
6. Every six months, repeat this time-control program. A good point here: After that first go-round, the repeats are much easier. Horrible week happens only once.

6.5 THE ACHIEVING ACTION

Everyone wants to go to Heaven . . . no one wants to die. Progressive college people want to be more productive . . . but they don't relish spending that unpleasant week of jotting down, minute by minute . . . all the things they do.

On the other hand . . . winners are people who do the things that losers don't like to do. The odds for winning increase sharply in favor of the individual who establishes his program. . . on a semi-annual basis . . . for all his working years.

SUCCESS EXERCISES

After having studied Chapter 6 you should be able to:

(1) Get more work done in less time

6-1   a. Prepare five copies of the DAILY "MINUTES" LOG as in Figure 6-1. One copy is to be used for each day of the week.
b. Review the part of this chapter pertaining to this figure.
c. Spend the next five work days completing the five forms, one for each day.
d. Have these forms typed so that your hurried notes are readable.

6-2   a. Prepare several copies of the TASK RECAP as shown in Figure 6-2.
b. Review in detail the completed "MINUTES" LOG to identify all tasks performed during

the week . . . list these on copies of Figure 6-2.
   c. Return to the "MINUTES" LOG and determine the number of times each task was performed and the total (or fractional) hours for each identified task.
   d. Have your results typed.

6-3 a. Prepare several copies of the TASK ANALYSIS form of Figure 6-3.
   b. Review in detail your TASK RECAP forms for specific tasks performed.
   c. On as many copies of Figure 6-3 as tasks identified, insert a specific TASK DESCRIPTION. Next answer each question as shown: for example, Who Else Can Do This? etc.

6-4 Place the completed forms of the above exercise in your ring binder. Review these often for points of self-improvement. You should repeat these exercises at least twice a year.

6-5 Have the people who report to you complete these exercises. Soon they will be able to get more work done in less time.

Chapter 7

Someone Should Do Something About Communications Around Here

"Establish a Weekly Status Report . . . Establish Weekly Communications Meetings . . . Roam"

INTRODUCTION: "I don't get enough information from my people," storms the president of the college.

"Nobody tells us anything," complain the department heads.

And from middle-management people, who have both superiors and subordinates: "The people don't tell me what I need to know . . . and the president locks himself in that ivory tower and tells me practically nothing."

All the people chorus: "Communications are lousy around here."

The nearest thing to a remedy is the not exactly hard-hitting proposal (offered by those who feel wronged by, but never wrong in communications) that "Someone should do something about communications around here."

True. Someone should. That someone should be the president. The president should strengthen communications in the college. But, if the president does not act, middle-management people should not (as too many do) sit on the backs of their laps and continue to bellyache.

A middle-management administrator can and should strengthen communications in his own area of control. When he does, he will find that his shining example of getting results through practical and simple techniques of communications will rub off on others. Other middle-management people will follow his lead, because there are and will always be those fearless administrators who have the "courage" to try anything that someone else made work, thus removing the risk.

In time, the president will jump on the band-wagon. Despite the many complaints about college presidents by their subordinates (most such complaints are largely unfounded, in that most secure middle-management people don't really know how windy it is up there in that tall, lonely tree of top management), it is just about always true that a president will adopt and follow a technique which he feels will make progress occur.

And sharp communications are progress-causing. Communications become progress-causing when the administrator realizes that it really isn't "communications" that is the objective. The objective is to get the results of good communications. The name of the game is not "communications." The name of the game is "progress."

Getting progress-causing communications doesn't require the study of bright and tempting techniques conjured up by speakers and writers who have never had to make communications make progress. There is always something missing in the teachings of a man who never was personally successful in doing the thing he talks and writes about.

One way of getting progress-causing communications is to use a technique already working successfully in many colleges (and the following technique qualifies) . . . and which is so simple and undemanding of time that the college doesn't need to substitute communications-learning time for getting-the-business-done time.

There are three steps to the simple and effectively technique of getting progress-causing communications. They are:

1. Establish a Weekly Status Report
2. Establish Weekly Communications Meetings
3. Roam

7.1 ESTABLISH A WEEKLY STATUS REPORT

L. Patrick Semicut is dean of Unnorris College. In response to the college president's bellowed command to "get your XXX in here," L. Patrick got in there.

"L. Patrick, how come I never know the things I need to know about the college?"

L. Patrick scratched his head. "I don't know, really. One reason, I think, is that we all seem too busy to talk to each other."

The president nodded. "True. Teaching and learning are heavy. Which is good. And I know you've got to recruit students. But I also know I need more information. I'll bet you do, too. L. Patrick, I'll bet you don't get enough information from your own people."

"That's right," L. Patrick admitted. "I'm carrying the same bag you are. Look. Let me noodle out a few thoughts on this and get back to you. Let me try to come up with something simple and workable."

Agreed. And L. Patrick, being a practical man, did come up with something simple and workable. L. Patrick came up with an incredible simple report (one side of one piece of paper). The piece of paper was a weekly status report as shown in Figure 7-1. The report, simple as a final product, was not so simple in design. It took much thought, much deep thought . . . before L. Patrick narrowed down all the things he thought should be communicated to the two things which are all that are really needed. The two things L. Patrick wanted to know from his subordinates, and which he wanted to tell his superior, were (1) Problems where help was needed and (2) Events of importance.

The president approved the form and L. Patrick put it into operation. In fact, the president, enthused, had all his management people put weekly status reports into effect. They did. And the result, as it always is in early states of communications paroxysms, was disaster.

In the beginning phases of weekly status reports, people will unburden their souls. They will report a huge backlog of problems and gripes which have built up over frustrating years of time. But the president knew this would happen. And he knew that, just by hanging in for three or four weeks, the weekly status reports would "level out" and would become both accurate in description and work-sized in remedy applications.

Expect weekly status reports to begin badly. But insist on getting them regularly and on time. After those first three or four weeks, it will be time to establish a follow-up . . . the weekly communications meetings.

7.2 ESTABLISH WEEKLY COMMUNICATIONS MEETINGS

"You started this thing, L. Patrick . . . so I want you to take the next step. After it works for you, we'll spread it around the college. In fact, as president, I'm going to fall into line, too.

NAME: DATE:
Problems Where I Need Help:
Events You Should Know About:

Figure 7-1. The Weekly Status Report Form

"Do this: Every Monday, for a half hour . . . and not a minute more . . . hold a meeting of your subordinates. Base the meeting on two things, L. Patrick. Number one, comment on the problems presented. Where you can solve them, do so. Where you can't promise answers and get answers . . . and report to your people at a later meeting."

"Number two, include on your agenda . . . and I want written agendas and I want to see copies . . . any particular item any of your people wants there . . . provided you agree they should be there. But make sure your people schedule into the agenda in advance, and not at the meeting. I don't want these meetings to degenerate into sudden-thought-and-endless-jabber sessions. We have too many of those as it is."

L. Patrick activated. The first three or four meetings, of a half hour each, did not cover all they should. But L. Patrick stuck to his half-hour limit, because Unnorris College just plain couldn't spare longer time not educating students. Then the meetings did become crisp and effective. The action points grew. The dreams and clerical peregrinations died out. The meetings worked. In a half hour. Communications improved dramatically.

The president was ready for the final fillip. He called L. Patrick in again.

7.3 ROAM

"L. Patrick, all our administrators are getting weekly status reports and are holding weekly communications meetings. As you know, I too am getting reports each week . . . from you and from the other people who run the college for me . . . and I'm holding my own weekly meetings with you. The results are good, and I'm glad we did this thing."

"Now, I want an added dimension. I want you (and after you, I'll have the others do this) to roam for thirty minutes every day."

L. Patrick looked up, surprised. "Roam?"

"Yes. Roam. I want you to leave your desk and prowl around among your people. I want you to ask each one, 'What are you thinking?' In the beginning, you'll get wise-guy answers. So keep your cool. Keep asking. One day one guy is going to discover that you really do want to know what he is thinking. And he'll tell you. He'll give you an idea."

"Then others will do the same. Many of their ideas won't work, but some of them will. And, who knows, one of these men (who maybe never had much to say before), just might one day snap back an answer that will double progress."

Roaming went as predicted. The wise-guy answers were plentiful (in fact, some were pretty funny, and L. Patrick later spoke about them at the local Rotary Club, which had tagged him for one of their programs). Then, following the wise-guy answers did come one, then two, then many expressions of thought. Some were ideas that worked.

One problem. The president, doing his own roaming, couldn't find L. Patrick. "Where is L. Patrick?" he asked. The answer: "Roaming." As he walked away, the president was heard to mutter: "Hoist on my own petard."

So far no one has dropped an idea which has doubled the progress of the college. But communications are sharp and progress is up. The name of the game didn't change, but the players got better.

7.4 ACHIEVING ACTION

Mr. Administrator, whatever your level, start this three-point communications program in your area of control. Persist with it, as you live through its initial failures. When your subordinates complain that "It won't work here," persist and prevail on them to hang in . . . to make the program work.

Better communications will improve the progress stature of any college. But you don't get "communications" by hoping for it and dreaming of it and complaining that someone should do something about it. Today, Mr. Administrator, would seem to be an excellent time (a bit late, perhaps, but an excellent time nonetheless) to activate your shot at this wonderful area of potential progress.

SUCCESS EXERCISES

After having studied Chapter 7 you should be able to:

(1) More effectively communicate in your college

7-1   Begin using the weekly status report of Figure 7-1 this week. Have it typed and on your superior's desk by noon Friday (or attach to an e-mail). Continue each week, hereafter, to forward the report . . . the first Friday you fail to turn it in do expect to have a call asking for it.

7-2   Have the people who work for you read this chapter. Then establish the procedure of their turning in the weekly status report to you by noon Friday . . . share with them copies of your weekly status report.

7-3   Establish a weekly communications meeting with your people to discuss their problems and relevant events.

7-4   Establish a pattern of "ROAMING" among your people. Before roaming, however, do read their weekly status reports and then respond to their specific needs.

Chapter 8

The Administrator's Professional Bibliography

"Read fifteen minutes each evening . . . Read four books at once . . . Use the Administrator's Bibliography as a training tool"

INTRODUCTION: By and large, successful college administrators are well read. There are too few exceptions to "read more, progress more" for ambitious men to chance being left out of the big-progress chase.

Unlike mastering most skills which lead to success, the establishment of a meaningful reading program is an easy and enjoyable way to make progress. Unlike mastering most skills, becoming a "professional progress-causing reader" doesn't require anything more than getting out and dusting off and applying an old habit.

In the process of formal education, referring particularly to high school and college, a man never read one book at a time! On the contrary, he was always reading on at least one book for each subject being studied . . . and for some subjects he was working on two or more books at the same time.

Indeed, in the high school and college atmosphere, it is not unusual to be reading six or eight or even ten books at the same time.

Some educators hold that this business of reading several books at a time gives each individual book more impact on the brain. They hold that a book, read against the background of other books, takes a more proper place in a man's "Professional Bibliography," in that balanced reading serves the whole man. . . rather than relieving a temporary cultural itch.

To revive and prosper from an old reading habit, three steps should be taken. They are:

1. Read fifteen minutes each evening
2. Read four books at once
3. Use the "Professional Bibliography" as a training tool

8.1 READ FIFTEEN MINUTES EACH EVENING

First, a commitment. A private commitment. First, a man's commitment to himself . . . that he will read at least fifteen minutes every evening. If he does, he will log five hundred hours a year in reading time. If he reads, on a program planned for both progress and pleasure, for five hundred hours a year . . . then he will add to his posture a complete extra education which will help drive him to the upper reaches of his ambition.

Bad arithmetic? Fifteen minutes per evening does not equal five hundred hours a year? Sure, it's bad arithmetic. But it's pretty good logic. Because, while there may be several fifteen-minute evening-reading increments, there will also be that evening when a man just can't put that book down. And those extra hours will produce a total of at least a solid five-hundred-hour reading year.

"L. Patrick, when are you coming to bed?"

"Just want to finish this chapter, dear."

One hour of silence.

"L. Patrick, aren't you coming to bed?"

"Soon. Just a few more pages."

Result: Three hours sleep. Cultural hangover in the morning. It happens to everybody. Better it should happen on purpose.

8.2 READ FOUR BOOKS AT ONCE

The four categories of books for professional-success reading are: (1) philosophy (2) specifics (3) measurement (4) balance. These categories are shown in Figure 8-1. The procedure is to read philosophy on Monday, specifics on Tuesday, measurement on Wednesday, balance on Thursday, back to philosophy on Friday, and so on. As a book is completed, it should be placed in the administrator's professional library and immediately replaced by another book in the same category. Thus, the administrator will enjoy a balanced reading lifetime . . . and will also build his Professional Bibliography.

Philosophy is "way to go." A philosophy book is a "what" book, not a "how" book. Philosophy gives the administrator direction toward progress. The book can be pure philosophy. Plato's *Republic* has a wealth of progress-idea triggers. Aristotle's points of view on excellence and perfection make a man nine feet tall . . . or it can be the inspiring *Think and Grow Rich*, by Napoleon Hill . . . or Auren Uris', *The Executive Breakthrough*. Or thousands of other books that a man may choose from this category.

Inspired by a powerful philosophy, an administrator activates that philosophy on the job. Thus, the next category: Specifics. This is a book written about the specifics of (1) the job the administrator is doing (2) the job the administrator plans to get next (he'll get it too, following this kind of program).

For accounting skills, the business officer might read *Accounting for Management and Planning and Control,* by Lynch.

The personnel manager might want to get with Marrow's *Making Management Human.*

The dean of instruction could do well to ponder *Holistic Literacy in College Teaching,* by John Rouche.

The president would find himself a bit sharper following his reading of Mary Zoglin's *Power of Politics in the Community College.*

Whatever the field, good books on specifics abound.

Having developed a philosophy, and having applied that philosophic force on the job, with specifics, there arises the natural question: How well is that job being done? Here the administrator must rate his results against a consistently high personal standard. No easy trick, that. Too often, a "hard day at the office" or a series of over-demanding situations, in addition to generating a to-heck-with-it-attitude, can put at least a temporary dent in a man's standard . . . will make him "settle for less."

How to stay high? Logically, staying high is to read about people who did just that . . . and who did it within the framework of situations at least as difficult as those faced by the administrator. Biographies. Autobiographies. Or fiction, where that fiction is well researched and is realistically based on the life of a great individual.

What individual? Well, one whom the administrator admires. A Lincoln man would read about Abraham Lincoln. A Benjamin Franklin man would read about Benjamin Franklin. Same ploy for the Napoleon man, the Churchill man, and so on. Certainly one of the finest books

PHILOSOPHY

1. *When I Say No, I Feel Guilty* .... M. Smith
2. *The Greatest Salesman In The World* .... Og Mandino
3. *The Prince* .... Niccolo Machiavelli
4. *Every Supervisor A Winner* .... Miller & Scott
5. *The Republic* .... Plato

SPECIFICS

1. *Management* .... Peter Drucker
2. *Increasing Individual Management Productivity* .... Hardesty & Scott
3. *The New Oratory* .... Anthony Jay
4. *Where Have All The Wooly Mammoths Gone?* .... Fred S. Frost
5. *Dress For Success* .... John T. Molloy

MEASUREMENT

1. *The Executive Breakthrough* .... Auren Uris
2. *I Don't Need You When I'm Right* .... Vic Gold
3. *Plain Speaking, An Oral Autobiography of Harry Truman* .... Merle Millar
4. *Six War Years* .... Barry Broadfoot
5. *A Man Called Intrepid* .... William Stephenson

BALANCE

1. *Marathon Man* .... J. Goldman
2. *A Cleft of Stars* .... Geoffry Jenkins
3. *Another Roadside Attraction* .... Tom Robbins
4. *Tai-Pan* .... James Clavell
5. *Running Blind* .... Desmond Bagley

Figure 8-1. Reading Program

on measurement is Irving Stone's *The Agony and the Ecstacy* . . . an inspiring treatment on a man (Michelangelo) whose drive and singleness of purpose achieved incredible results. With Michelangelo's make-up, no administrator can be stopped (delayed, yes . . . stopped, no) anywhere short of his goal.

The fourth and final category is balance. It is exactly that. This is a book which has absolutely nothing to do with college business. It is for sheer pleasure. Hedonistic, if you will. In some cases, you can obtain these books with plain covers!

8.3 USE THE ADMINISTRATOR'S PROFESSIONAL BIBLIOGRAPHY AS A TRAINING TOOL

When an administrator follows the four-books-at-a-time technique, his library grows quickly. And it grows with directions, too, being tied in to the objectives of his college, which are naturally relevant to his own directions. Soon, in his normal contacts with his subordinates, the administrator will find that much of his professional bibliography (the growing list of books on which much of his success is based) is good for them, too. He will discern, from time to time, problems of subordinates' future advancements.

"Dr. Unnorris. I'm frustrated. As you know, I'm not a Ph.D. And I see young guys coming into the college from time to time . . . and getting pretty good deals. I'm not mad about it. I know you need what these guys have. What bugs me is that the higher jobs here don't seem to need what I have. I think I'm stuck."

The slow smile of confidence crept over the administrator's face. "Seemore, I'm glad you brought that up. Because I don't think you're stuck at all. Look . . . I've noticed that you're doing a pretty good job running the bookstore . . . meeting those mission impossible deadlines where book salesmen promise the moon, with a few stars thrown in. So let's take a higher look. Let's consider that you might be able to advance as an auxiliary services coordinator."

"Do this, Seemore. Read Crisp's 'Sales Planning and Control.' It's part of my professional bibliography, and I'll get it to you tomorrow. Read it close and well. Then make a 'book report' to me. If I think you make sense, then I'll try to make sense on where you're going in this college."

As the administrator's library grows, so grows the number of opportunities he has to match his subordinates' ambitions with the professional bibliography. A good leader already, he becomes the better manager of men whose objectives are consistent with college directions . . . at the same time leaving those men free to operate as fearless individuals within those directions. And he will, beyond doubt, inspire a number of his men to develop the four-book reading habit . . . and to begin to build their own professional bibliographies.

8.4 THE ACHIEVING ACTION

The action point is to buy and begin reading those first four books. The timing is today. Progress will be immediately discernible. The growing posture of the administrator will clamor for more and more notice. He is destined for success, because no force can stop the man who has a thing he must do and who helps his own cause by being a professional progress-causing reader.

SUCCESS EXERCISES

After having studied Chapter 8 you should be able to:

(1) Establish a professional reading program for yourself

8-1   Make a copy of Figure 8-1. Complete your own special listing within each category. If you need help in selecting books...ask your associates. . .check , www.amazon.com or www.1stbooks.com .

8-2   Now purchase or borrow or check out of the library the first book listed for each category . . . select your own balance book. You now have four books. Begin by reading fifteen minutes of philosophy on the first night, fifteen minutes of specifics on the second night, and so on. When you have read all of the books you have listed on Figure 8-1, your professional reading habits will have been established.

8-3   Prepare a form similar to Figure 8-2. On it, list the titles of books you are presently reading. The first three books should be those listed for the three categories of your reading program of Figure 8-1. It is not necessary that you list your balance book.

8-4   Each time you see or hear of a book you wish to read, list it on your professional bibliography. This action will eliminate your having forgotten the title by the time you get around to reading it. Each three months set an objective for yourself as to how many books you will read from your listing.

8-5 Have the people who work for you complete these exercises. Soon everyone within your control will have established a professional reading program. It is a fact that most of our learning comes from reading.

ADMINISTRATIVE BIBLIOGRAPHY

1. *When I Say No, I Feel Guilty* .... M. Smith

2. *The Greatest Salesman In The World* .... Og Mandino

3. *Fast Forward Leadership* .... Louellen Essex

4. *The Leadership Moment* .... Michael Useem

5. *The Executive Breakthrough* .... Auren Uris

6. *A Man Called Intrepid* .... William Stephenson

7. *Marathon Man* .... J. Goldman

8. *Another Roadside Attraction* .... Tom Robbins

9. *Understanding Leadership Competencies* .... Pat Guggenheimer

10. Etc.

Figure 8-2. The Administrative Bibliography

Chapter 9

How to Make an Eloquent Speech

"The college administrator is an eloquent speaker, though he rarely knows it. By being in his 'natural habitat' when at the lectern, the administrator will discover and progress from his eloquence."

INTRODUCTION: An effective administrator, at his job, is exciting to behold. He seems to be doing all these things at the same time:

1. Answering the phone. . .keeping the discussion crisp and short . . .deciding
2. Greeting a visitor. . .making the visitor happy. . . getting on with things to be done
3. Analyzing paper . . . deciding
4. Thinking . . . deciding

The effective administrator is not only exciting to behold, and to work with . . . but he is himself excited. There, behind his desk, in his natural habitat . . . coolly controlling a high volume of people flow and paper flow. Despite his frequent sharp remonstrances and growls of impatience . . . he is highly enjoying himself.
  He is in control. He is in his natural habitat.
  He is master of all he surveys.

Then one day he learns that he must make a speech. Turnaround: The tiger becomes a pussy-cat. He worries while he plans his speech (and he over plans mightily) . . . he continues to worry right up to the time he reaches the lectern (which he calls a "podium" . . . and it isn't) . . . then delivers a stilted speech that justifies every minute of the worrying he did.

Yet, the stumbling speaker up there is not the bumbler he appeared to be. On the contrary, he really is a top administrator. He really does pull in a hefty eighty or ninety or more per year. And he really is worth every cent of what he's paid. In short, the audience really is looking at and listing to an administrator. But the speaker is not looking or sounding like an administrator.

Things simply don't need to be that way. The college administrator, when making a speech, can put forth every bit of his powerful image . . . can come across as well, or better, than he does on the job. In two simple steps. These steps are:

1. Recreate the natural habitat.
2. Have a "reverse question-and-answer period."

9.1 RECREATE THE NATURAL HABITAT

What is the "natural habitat" of the administrator? Answer: The atmosphere in which he is at his best.

What is this atmosphere? Answer: The administrator is at his best when he is at his desk . . . providing for one of his associates in need . . . an answer to one of those few mind-boggling and difficult questions that works its way up to the administrator's level.

The administrator revels in his ability to unravel these Gordian knots. Not that he always unravels them. Often, he attacks the problem the same way Alexander the Great attacked the original Gordian knot. He simply cuts the rope.

But, whatever he does . . . this is where the administrator is at his best. And it's what he enjoys most. And it's the reason why he often hates to make speeches!

Because, when he is at the lectern, the administrator knows he is not at his best. Even if his lectern performance would not be still and stilted, still . . . it would be far less impressive than if he were in his natural habitat . . . behind his desk . . . handling those tough questions.

Therefore, to show the administrator at his best . . . when at the lectern . . . it is simply a case of recreating his natural habitat. Not by bringing his desk to the speaker location, like a security blanket or rubber duckie . . . rather, by setting up the same question-and-answer condition.

Here, then, are the steps the administrator should take, in preparing for his speech. He should think up, then write down . . . the questions he feels the audience would want to ask about his subject. For example, supposing the administrator has been asked to make a luncheon speech to the local civic club.

Now . . . what would the audience want to know about the local college or university? What would their questions be? These questions could be, using the Who-What-Where-When-Why-How question starters:

1. Who are your students?
2. What types of educational programs do you provide your students?
3. Where do the students come from within the community?

4. When do the prospective students need to apply for admission?
5. Why is the education that your college provides a good investment for the student . . . the community and industry within the college service area?
6. How do you intend to provide increased services within the community?

And those questions are the speech. Indeed, the administrator may never get by the first one. Because here's what can happen when he will have a reverse questions-and-answer period.

9.2 HAVE A REVERSE QUESTION-AND-ANSWER PERIOD

The administrator is at the lectern. He has been introduced. All he has up there is a piece of paper listing his six questions. He faces his audience. He says, in his own words, and not reading:

"Ladies and Gentlemen, I am pleased to be with you today. And, though I won't speak for a very long while . . . I will be different."

"The difference is that my entire speech will be a question-and-answer period. And that isn't the only difference."

"The next difference is that, in this question-and-answer period, I will ask the questions. In doing so, I've noddled out what I think are the questions you'd want to ask about Unnorris College."

"The first question I think you'd ask is this: 'Who are your students?'"

Now the administrator is in his natural habitat. He has just received a question. Not even a tough question. With confident mien, he moves away from the lectern. . . looks at his audience... smiles. . .and does what comes naturally. He answers.

He glows. He exudes. His enthusiasm is infectious. He is not "reading a speech."

After the few minutes it takes for his answer, he pauses. He asks his audience: "Do you have another question?"

Chances are they will. If so, he answers. And he keeps answering until his time is up. But, at any point . . if the audience does not quickly produce a question . . . he has his six, quite enough to cover far more than his allotted time.

Problem: This technique is so effective that the administrator could make a major mistake. He could talk too long. And this he must not do. Ever.

How to control finishing time? Easy. Be it in the middle of a sentence, or whenever . . . when it is time to stop . . . stop! It's done this way:

The administrator looks at his watch. He feigns surprise. He says: "Well, seems my time is up. So I'll stop. No problem, really. There can be no following questions-and-answer period. We just had one. In fact, that's all we had. I hope you enjoyed it as much as I."

And sit. And enjoy the applause. It will be resounding applause. And once done, the administrator has that wonderful feeling unique to a speaker who has, in the all-important minds of his listeners, done a proper job.

The administrator did not become an eloquent speaker that day. Because he was always an eloquent speaker. It's just that he didn't find out he was that good . . . until that day.

The administrator can . . . and will . . . take it from there. Indeed, he'll find a way to get his eloquence on his bottom line.

Because the bottom line is the logical resting place for whatever the administrator does well.

9.3 THE ACHIEVING ACTION

So, Mr. College Administrator, do start putting forth every bit of your powerful image. Examine Figure 9-1 for other questions that might apply to any subject of a natural habitat speech.

You should construct other questions on Figure 9-2.

SUCCESS EXERCISES

After having studied Chapter 9 you should be able to

(1) Make public speeches using the "natural habitat" approach

9-1 Make a copy of Figure 9-2. Write in a subject that you feel competent to give a speech on. You may best relate the subject to what you do on your job or maybe services your college provides.

9-2 Write your speech plan for the subject. You may wish to change the questions after the key words WHO, WHAT, WHERE, WHEN, WHY and HOW of Figure 9-1.

9-3   Now practice your speech plan. Practice in the privacy of your room . . . in front of the mirror!

9-4   Give your speech to an appropriate audience.

9-5   Were you able to give your speech as described within this chapter? If not, then ask yourself the question, why?

SUBJECT:	
Who will benefit from knowledge of "subject?"	
What is most important thing to do in order to make "subject" work?	
Where is "subject" best applied?	
When does "subject" work best?	
How does one go about learning more about "subject?"	
Describe cases, from experience, where "subject" worked well.	

Figure 9-1. Other Natural Habitat Speech Questions

SUBJECT:	

Figure 9-2. Natural Habitat Speech Form

Chapter 10

How to Write a Policy

"A policy exists when a question is never asked twice."

INTRODUCTION: "What we have around here are duplicated decisions." So complained Dr. Unnorris. "We must be wasting a heckuva lot of time."

How so, Dr. Unnorris?

"People come in here for what are loosely termed business discussions: lighting pipes, babbling what passes for masculine humor and, occasionally, a decision gets made."

Dr. Unnorris, I'm sure you can control the time-wasting. Then you can get more decisions in less time. You can get those decisions made . . . progress-causing points covered.

"That's not the way I see the problem. Way I see the problem is this: I don't mind a little arm wrestling in the discussion. These guys work hard, need to let off a little steam. So let'em tell a few dirty jokes, and blow smoke all over my office."

"I think where the time is wasted is in the decision process itself. I see hours of discussion leading to decisions that, once made, are too darned familiar."

"What I mean is this: Those decisions were made before. We're making the same decisions over and over again. This has got to be a great time-waster."

Your point is well taken, Dr. Unnorris.

"Of course it is."

I think we can do something about the problem.

"If by 'do something' you mean you have a specific proposal to make . . . fine. Otherwise, we're wasting time right now."

I have a specific proposal to make, Dr. Unnorris.

"Good. Do it."

Okay. First off, let's begin with the premise that heads up this chapter: "A policy exists when a question is never asked twice." Do we agree on that premise, Dr. Unnorris?

"We sure do. One hundred percent."

Now let's take a look at the condition of most written policies in the college or university. I'll tick off those conditions for you:

NUMBER ONE: NOTHING EXISTS IN WRITING

College people defend this condition with a comment such as: "We don't need a written policy. We know what policy is. Anyway, that stuff is confidential. We don't want that information rattling around where everyone could see it."

But in real life . . . these people don't know policy. Without written policy, no two people have the same understanding of an issue. If "we know what policy is" is an accurate statement . . . then, that which people know can hardly be called "confidential."

NUMBER TWO: THE SCATTERED-MEMO SYNDROME

This is similar to the approach used in Hawaii's salad days. Every now and then the head Hawaiian would dream up a new law . . . and announce it. And everyone had better remember.

In the college community, the head honcho thinks up a new rule and dashes off a memo. Some people keep these memos in files. Some toss the memos into a desk drawer. Some people make mental notes and throw the memos away.

But nowhere can be found an indexed complete set of updated written policies.

NUMBER THREE: THE OBSOLETE WRITTEN POLICY

Here the college does have a written policy. The policy is written, approved, indexed . . . and distributed to the proper people. But, once written . . . the policy is left that way.

Conditions changed, but the policy did not change. Sure, the policy reflected past conditions. But it did not reflect current conditions. The policy was obsolete.

The need is for a policy that is always current . . . and which can be established and maintained at low cost. My proposal comes in ten steps. Those steps are:

1. Select areas needing written policies
2. Define "policy" and "procedure"
3. Establish the "question and answer" approach
4. Involve the people
5. Obtain questions and proposals
6. Consolidate questions and proposals
7. Establish policies and procedures
8. Create and distribute policy manual
9. Update
10. Review

10.1 SELECT AREAS NEEDING WRITTEN POLICIES

Here you determine the areas of your college which need written policies. Use major functional classifications, such as "Financial Management" . . . "Public Relations" . . . "Data Processing" . . .

"Personnel" . . . "Student Services" . . . and so on. For purposes of this explanation, I'll use "Purchasing Policy" as the base.

"I kind of thought you would."

Why, Dr. Unnorris?

"Because you look a little like a vulture."

Purchasing agents are not vultures, Dr. Unnorris.

"What the heck are they, then?"

Barracudas.

"Okay. Okay. Get on with it."

10.2 DEFINE "POLICY" AND "PROCEDURE."

A policy is "how to do it."

A procedure is "what to do."

Under the written policy will be the written step-by-step procedure. For example:

> POLICY: The Purchasing Department may purchase for the using department a specific manufacturer's model number, thus eliminating all competition.

> PROCEDURE:
>
> 1. When it is necessary to request quotations on a special brand name and model number,

2. the statement "NO SUBSTITUTES WILL BE CONSIDERED" will be included with the specifications.
3. "NO SUBSTITUTE" requisitions will be justified with an attached memorandum from the division director to the director of purchasing, explaining in detail why no other competitive brand is acceptable.
4. The memorandum will be APPROVED and countersigned BY THE AREA VICE PRESIDENT.

10.3 ESTABLISH THE "QUESTION AND ANSWER" APPROACH

Put into your mind, Dr. Unnorris . . . that a policy is written from a "Question and Answer Period."

"Like after a speech? Like asking questions after the speaker finishes?"

Exactly, Dr. Unnorris.

"Best part of the speech it is, too. Usually, the guy reads his speech. Dull. But he can't read answers to questions. Best part of the speech. Only good part of most of them, in fact. But, okay . . . I've put into my mind that a policy is a written Question and Answer Period. What next?"

Next, Dr. Unnorris . . . comes Step 4.

10.4 INVOLVE THE PEOPLE

Write a memo to all the people who are involved, directly or indirectly, with the question to be answered . . .

the area of policy need. The memo I propose is Figure 10-1.

"Looks okay to me."

Do you approve the memo, Dr. Unnorris?

"Yes. And . . . you did it again?"

What did I do?

"You wrote the whole darned thing without using a word of more than three syllables."

That's my memo-writing style, Dr. Unnorris.

"Don't get chesty."

10.5 OBTAIN QUESTIONS AND PROPOSALS

On the last working day of next month, L. Pat will receive the questions and proposed answers. He'll then proceed as explained in Figure 10-1.

"Okay."

10.6 CONSOLIDATE QUESTIONS AND PROPOSALS

Again, L. Pat will proceed as explained in Figure 10-1.

"Right."

10.7 ESTABLISH POLICIES AND PROCEDURES

And, once again, L. Pat will proceed as explained in Figure 10-1.

DATE:	04/25/20xx
TO:	As Listed
FROM:	L. Patrick Semicut, Dean
SUBJECT:	Instructional Policy
OBJECTIVE:	To establish and maintain Instructional Policy
WHY:	At present, too many policies exist in the form of loose memos . . . and thoughts in people's minds. Also, many needed policies don't exist at all.
	The lack of policies means that the same questions are asked and answered over and over again. A complete written policy will (1) keep us all on the same track, and (2) save time on those repeated questions and answers.
	A policy exists when no question needs to be asked twice. But we surely do need all the questions to be asked once.
	Thus, the following course of action:
COURSE OF ACTION:	
You 1.	Write all questions, to which you need answers, in relation to our instructional policies. Write these questions (a) as they exist in your mind right now, and (b) as they occur on the job, in the next thirty days.

Figure 10-1. Memo To Your People Initiating Policy Writing Procedure

You	2.	Where you feel you have answers to your own questions, propose such answers. If we can, we'll use your answers as policies.
You	3.	Thirty days from today, on x/xx/xx . . . place your questions and proposed answers on my desk.
	4.	On receipt of your data, I will: A. Combine duplicate questions and proposed answers B. Create answers, from my knowledge, or C. Obtain answers, where I am uncertain D. Obtain approval of answers (they'll be in the form of written policies and procedures) E. Issue the Instructional-Policy Manual
You	5.	After you have submitted your questions and proposed answers... continue listing questions and **proposed answers not yet in the Instructional-Policy Manual.** Place those questions and proposed answers on my desk on the last working day of every quarter.

Figure 10-1 Continued

6. On receipt of more questions and proposed answers, I will perform as in Step 4. You'll receive those added policies and procedures, to place in the Instructional-Policy Manual.
7. Every year, the entire Instructional-Policy Manual will be read and re-approved and/or edited . . . by the Executive Committee of the college. Changes that stem from quarterly re-approvals (to assure that we keep pace with changing conditions) will be given to you, for updating the Instructional-Policy Manual.

GUIDANCE: To guide your approach (but surely not to influence your thinking) . . . here are examples of questions you might ask.

. . . Who makes the final decision on course of program placement that will offer the student a reasonable chance of success?

. . . When will each classroom instructor be provided a list of students enrolled for each course?

. . . Under what conditions can course prefixes and numbers within the college course numbering system be changed?

. . . What is the procedure for changing courses within the college curriculum?

Thank you for helping us build and maintain the Instructional-Policy Manual.

Figure 10-1 Continued

"But, I don't think he'll know all those answers."

No doubt of that, Dr. Unnorris. Where he doesn't have the answer, he'll get the data he needs. His sources will be:

- A. Other instructional deans around the state. These people meet every quarter . . . are quite friendly. The synergy of their combined brains will get many answers.
- B. People right here in the college. You. Me. Division deans. Department heads. Faculty.

When he gets his answers, L. Pat will then run them by the Administrative Council for final approval.

10.8   CREATE AND DISTRIBUTE POLICY MANUAL

When L. Pat gets his editions and/or approvals, he'll be ready to put his pages together. He will:
- A. Determine titles for the various parts of the manual
- B. Use those titles in indexes
- C. Have policies and procedures placed in the indexed portions
- D. Have copies of the Instructional-Policy Manual reproduced
- E. Distribute copies of the manual to all involved people

"Okay."

10.9 UPDATE

The Instructional-Policy Manual is updated by continuing questions and proposals. These are submitted on the last working day of every quarter, by involved people. Figure 10-1 gives the details.

10.10 REVIEW

The entire Instructional-Policy Manual is reviewed yearly. (Refer back to Figure 10-1 for details.)

10.11 THE ACHIEVING ACTION

Establishing a viable and dynamic policy is a simple task. The ten steps are simple.

But, a warning: There is a big bulge of long and hard work in there. That bulge happens when the project leader is snowed under by that plethora of paper which will funnel to his desk . . . when that first batch of questions and proposed answers comes in.

Consolidating the duplications. Writing and finding answers to questions. This is a tremendous task.

But only once. Just once. Once that first big bulge is taken care of, the project will never again be long and hard work. Because the coming monthly additions will be in small volume.

"I think it's a good thing to tell people, before they take on a project of this scope . . . that there'll be what you call a 'bulge of long and hard work.'"

Cuts down later complaints, Dr. Unnorris.

"It does something else, too. I think it tells the people who will take on this work that I'm making note of who they are."

Making note, Dr. Unnorris? What do you mean?

"I mean anyone who completes a policy project around here is going to get a green X on his forehead. Now you probably want to know what a green X is."

That I do, Dr. Unnorris.

"Well, when I see someone who I think is going to succeed in this college, I put a green X on his forehead. That means this guy or gal is on the move."

"When I see somebody who is not to be promoted, I slap on a red X."

"Some people don't have any X's. Yet. Because I haven't decided. But I will. In time, everybody gets an X."

"The people with the X's can't see them. But I can see them. And I run this college."

Seems to me, Dr. Unnorris, that all colleges have people who give X's and people who get X's.

"Absolutely true. And the game is to get a green X."

I wonder if I have an X, Dr. Unnorris.

"You do."

I wonder what color.

"I want to keep you wondering about that."

SUCCESS EXERCISES

After having studied Chapter 10 you should be able to activate the following Soppada:

SUBJECT: Policy

OBJECTIVE: To establish and maintain a policy that is always current

PRESENT SITUATION: Most policies exist in phantom form. Others, when specific . . . are often obsolete.

PROPOSAL: That the administrator shall establish and maintain, for his area of control . . . written policies that are always current. The major steps are:

1. Select areas needing written policies
2. Define "policy" and "procedure"
3. Establish the "question and answer" approach
4. Involve the people
5. Obtain questions and proposals
6. Consolidate questions and proposals
7. Establish policies and procedures
8. Create and distribute policy manual
9. Update
10. Review

ADVANTAGES:

1. <u>TIME SAVING</u>. "How to do it" questions are asked only once. Much time is saved in eliminating duplicate discussions.

2. <u>MOTIVATION</u>. The people who do the work are legitimately involved in building the policies. And people are motivated to pursue a course, when they are in on the origination of that course.

3. <u>WINNING</u>. Your competitor is probably still flailing away with phantom policies. Your written program gives you a competitive edge.

DISADVANTAGES:

1. <u>TIME LOST</u>. Some key people are going to spend a great amount of time in building the policy. However, that time is spent only once. In the long run, much time is <u>saved</u>.

2. <u>HURT FEELINGS</u>. Many people like to "wing it." With solid policies in effect, winging is out. However, working within established policies will separate the pros from the amateurs. If some people's feelings are hurt, do help them update their resumes. Be kind.

<u>ACTION</u>: Today, you . . . for your area of control . . . sell policy level on your heading up the project of establishing a written policy.

Chapter 11

How to Assert Authority

"When the college administrator recognizes his breadth of authority, he will be highly successful."

INTRODUCTION: Dr. Unnorris wore a challenging expression. "Who the heck are 'they'?"

Pardon me?

"When people around here say 'they' can't get anything done . . . who the heck are 'they'?"

I suppose "they" are, to me, all people except myself. But I don't sense you are digging for a literal definition here. Just what is on your mind, Dr. Unnorris?

"Let me relate this to something that happens too often around here:"

"A project is assigned. Work takes place. Meetings happen.

Memos proliferate. By deadline date, the project isn't completed properly."

"When I check into this with someone, I get the excuse, 'I could get this thing done if they would only give me the authority.'"

"For all I know, the excuse is valid. Maybe we don't delegate enough authority around here. Indeed, maybe I'm the 'they' people complain about. What do you think?"

Dr. Unnorris, I think the people heading up and working on the projects do have all the authority needed. The excuse is not valid.

"If that's true, then I'd better get the point across to our people. But before that, you'd better get the point across to me, because I don't know what you're talking about."

"I imagine you're ready to explain all this to me."

I certainly am, Dr. Unnorris.

"Okay. Let's have it."

Right, Dr. Unnorris. To understand what authority really is, we need to take three steps. Those three steps are:

1. Put authority into two frames of reference
2. Expand authority into four dimensions
3. Activate four-dimensional authority

11.1 PUT AUTHORITY INTO TWO FRAMES OF REFERENCE

Take a look at Figure 11-1, Dr. Unnorris. Two frames of reference. You'll see . . . first . . . "Responsibility." That's the biggest area.

Within "Responsibility" is a smaller area: "Accountability." Then comes the smallest area. . .and our subject. . . "Authority."

Let's define those three words, beginning with the biggest area: "Responsibility." I take a different view of that word, I may be wrong, but I don't define "Responsibility" as many others do.

"You don't do most things the way other people do. Sometimes I think you have a wheel off the ground."

Quite possible, Dr. Unnorris. But, if I may continue . . . I am going to beef up your bottom line on progress with my full explanation.

"Responsibility"

"Accountability"

"Authority"

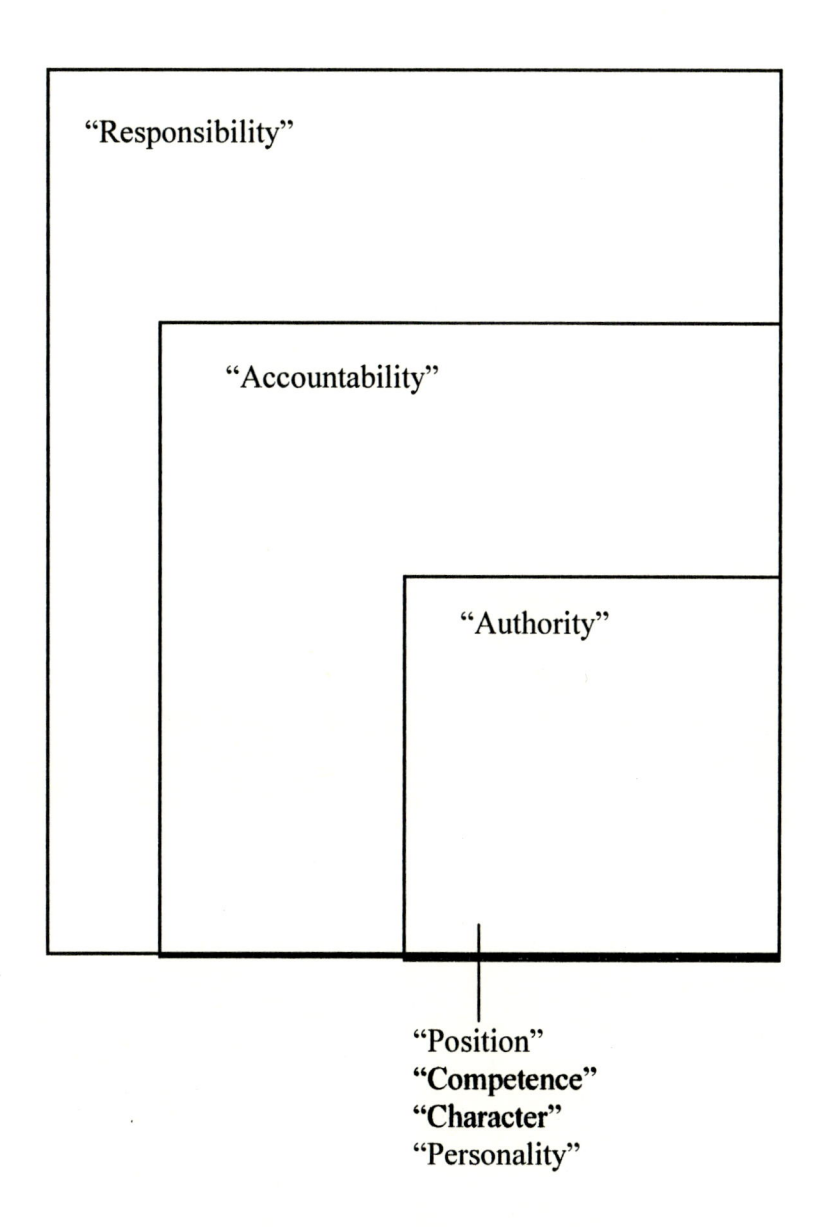

"Position"
"Competence"
"Character"
"Personality"

Figure 11-1. Two Frames of Reference for Authority

"Bottom line on progress? Magic words. Continue."

Dr. Unnorris, I think "Responsibility" is a private thing. I don't think it's a thing someone gives. I don't think "Responsibility" is properly defined on a position or job specification. I don't think "Responsibility" is a feeling. I think it is closely related to (and perhaps the same thing as) "Ambition."

I've heard people, maybe at the department head level . . . way below presidential level . . . people who feel bad when a bad thing happens to the college . . . and who feel good when a good thing happens to the college.

Now these people aren't responsible for the events that made either bad or good things happen. Far from it. But these people feel responsible.

I think the feeling is triggered by their ambitions . . . and these ambitions may be subconscious, or maybe not . . . their ambitions to one day be on the upper administrative level, perhaps even to replace you, Dr. Unnorris.

"Not in my lifetime will I be replaced."

Maybe not, Dr. Unnorris. But this college will live longer than you.

"It sure will. Good point. I was the founding President."

I know that, Dr. Unnorris. To continue: I believe that "Responsibility" is "Ambition." On Figure 11-1, it's a big area. For some people. For people who want to be responsible.

An area smaller than "Responsibility," but within its parameters . . . is "Accountability." That area is more vague than most people think it is, but I'm certain I have "Accountability" defined properly.

"Accountability" is that which the boss expects of the subordinate. As with "Responsibility," you won't find a clear description of "Accountability" in a position or job specification. You won't find it in a memo. You won't hear it in a discussion. You discover it this way: You work under an administrator two to three years. You get to know the boss.

You get to feel what the boss expects. And feelings baffle words. Feelings are ineffable. But feelings are accurate, very accurate. You feel, accurately, what the boss does and does not expect.

You are accountable to fill the boss' expectations.

"I think your wheels are all on the ground at this point. I know I've felt my own frustration at my inability to get across to people what I expect. I'm sure I never said it or wrote it properly. But I know what I expect and my better people seem to know."

Which brings us to "Authority," Dr. Unnorris . . . that little area within "Accountability." Here's my definition of "Authority" . . . . "That which one can do without getting approval from a higher level."

As an example, Dr. Unnorris . . . let's take L. Patrick Semicut, one of our good upper management people . . . our dean of the college.

"L. Pat. Yes. He's a good one."

Now. L. Pat is not on the presidential-trustee level. So, he does not have the authority to establish new policies. But he does have the authority to propose a policy change.

L. Pat does not have the authority to replace your schedule of tuition charges with a new one. But he does have the authority to recommend to you a different schedule of tuition charges.

L. Pat does not have the authority to make a speech at your monthly Trustee's Board Meeting to express the college's long range plans. But he does have the authority, in talking on his own subjects, to make the best darned speech on the program.

"He did, too . . . at the last Board meeting. L. Pat was good at that lectern."

He wasn't quite the best, Dr. Unnorris.

"What do you mean?"

I spoke on that program, Dr. Unnorris.

"Oh, boy. Let's get on with this."

Dr. Unnorris, let's get back to the complaint we discussed before. A complaint which should be recognition of a golden opportunity for advancement. You'll recall that your voicing of that oft-heard complaint was: "I could get this thing done if they would only give me the authority."

"You've come back to my complaint, word for word. And I like your frames of reference. But I don't have my answer. Where is all this authority you said our people already have?"

That brings us to Step Two, Dr. Unnorris.

11.2 EXPAND AUTHORITY INTO FOUR DIMENSIONS

Dr. Unnorris, I'm going back to that "golden opportunity" I mentioned before. The complaint was: "I could get this thing done if they would only give me the authority." The golden opportunity is this:

A major measurement of an administrator's performance is that which he can get done without clearly defined authority. Indeed, I've know many top people (and you are one of them) who assign beyond-authority projects in order to see how the receiver conducts himself.

"You're right. I do. But what's all this 'he' and 'him?' We have women administrators around here."

I know we do, Dr. Unnorris. You'll recall that the Federal Government required us to put women in better jobs in order to keep our federal funds.

"Fact remains, they are here. What's with all the 'he' and 'him' you keep saying?"

Grammar, Dr. Unnorris.

"Grammar?"

Sure. In the English language, it is proper grammar . . . when referring to both men and women . . . to use the masculine third person. Doing that does not make me a misogynist.

"A what?"

Misogynist. That's the official word for "male chauvinist pig."

"I don't know why I walk into these traps. Now . . . let's get back to the 'golden opportunity.' What do you mean?"

It's the opportunity for the administrator to expand his authority from one dimension (to which many limit themselves) to four dimensions (to which all should expand themselves).

In looking at authority, too many consider only one dimension: the authority of position. And a very real authority that is, too. The authority of position holds that the department head reports to the division chairman . . . the division chairman to the dean of the college . . . the dean of the college to the vice president . . . the vice president to the president.

While we are not always happy with the people in those jobs, still . . . we must have the discipline and organization that is the authority of position. The buck must stop somewhere. Decisions must often be made to deadlines. Colleges need the authority of position.

But there are three other dimensions of authority. And when the administrator develops all three, he will frequently overcome the authority of his boss . . . within existing policies, and with the approval (more than approval, the blessing) of the boss.

Refer back to Figure 11-1. Notice the arrow from "Authority." That arrow points to the words describing the four dimensions of authority. The first word is "Position." We covered that. The other three dimensions are "Competence", "Character" and "personality." Let's cover those dimensions.

Let's say that Al reports to Mary. Has, for two or three years. Al's objective has been, and is . . . to be Mary's most competent subordinate. Al has worked diligently to be number one to Mary and, indeed . . . Mary does judge Al to be her most competent subordinate.

Al approaches Mary. "Mary, I've worked out an idea. I think it'll make some progress around here. I'd like ten minutes of your time, to run this by you."

Even before Mary hears the idea, she wants to say "yes." She wants to go along with her most competent subordinate. Now, Mary isn't about to approve a bad idea . . .but she doesn't expect a bad idea from her most competent subordinate.

Al, therefore, has an edge . . . an authority . . . over Mary, with Mary's approval . . . and well within policy. That's the authority of "Competence." And it isn't enough.

Al must also have the authority of "Character." It works this way:

In the two or three years that she has been Al's boss, Mary has noticed two business sins that Al does not commit:

> 1. Al never stole from her, in terms of either money or time (pretty much the same thing).
>
> 2. Al never lied to her.

Let's take a hard look at item two above. It does not mean that Al never said a wrong thing to Mary. On the contrary, he said several wrong things. Those wrong things were not lies. They were mistakes. And Mary no doubt called Al in for a word of prayer about each mistake. But Al didn't lie and he didn't steal.

And Al wants to present an idea to Mary. Even before Mary hears the idea, she very much wants to approve. She wants very much to bestow a resounding "yes" on a subordinate of high competence and high character. Attaining those two dimensions, Al surely has a very real edge on overcoming Mary's authority of position . . . within existing policies . . . with the approval of the boss.

And that is still not enough. Because Al must also have the authority of "Personality."

"Personality? Heck, I can see through some of those fast-talk personality people in two seconds. What kind of authority is that?"

By itself, Dr. Unnorris . . . it is nothing. But, when combined with the other two authorities, it makes Al almost irresistible to Mary. Works this way:

Al asks Mary to spare ten minutes to listen to an idea. But Mary is tied up. Tight. "How about 9 a.m. tomorrow, my office?" Mary proposes. Al agrees.

That evening, when he goes home . . . Al takes all the data which will support his next-day oral presentation. That evening, at home . . . he practices the presentation: voice variance and hand motions, which he learned at Toastmaster Club (the best place I know to learn how to express oneself) . . . crisp and succinct articulation . . . etc. Al puts forth every facet of his personality.

Mary is no dummy. Next day, in hearing Al's presentation...she notices the special selling voice, hand motions, whatever. But, because Mary regards Al to be competent and of high character . . . she knows that the histrionics are not for self-aggrandizement. She knows the promotion of personality is done to express Al's deep belief in the idea, and what the idea will do to help the college.

Thus, personality . . . combined with character and competence . . . make Al almost irresistible to Mary. Al has overcome the authority of position with the approval of his boss...and within college policy.

11.3   ACTIVATE FOUR-DIMENSIONAL AUTHORITY

The first step in putting four-dimensional authority to work is to merely recognize that every college person is able to master all four dimensions.

Anyone can become competent. Competence is gained through the studying done and effort put forth to do that job better than anybody else can do it.

Character is easy. While you and I may be less than saintly in the conduct of our personal lives, we'll surely earn a college halo when we don't lie and don't steal.

Personality? We all have it. All it takes is to exploit those special abilities we discover in ourselves.

Position? That dimension of authority comes to us when we activate the other three.

11.4   THE ACHIEVING ACTION

That high college position doesn't come next Tuesday. Takes awhile. But it will surely come to the activator of four-dimensional authority.

Then you and I won't need to be concerned about who "they" are.

Because they will be us.

SUCCESS EXERCISES

After having studied Chapter 11 you should be able to activate the following Soppada:

SUBJECT: Authority

OBJECTIVE: To attain success through recognizing and activating four-dimensional authority

PRESENT SITUATION: Most administrators see authority in only one dimension, thus limiting potential.

PROPOSAL: Attain the above objective in three steps:
1. Put authority into two frames of reference
2. Expand authority into four dimensions
3. Activate four-dimensional authority

ADVANTAGES:

1. NO RANCOR. Broader authority is activated without incurring rancor. Indeed, the boss approves the action.

2. NO POLICY VIOLATION. Broader authority is activated within existing policy. This may be the only way for the administrator to be a "swinger" within policy.

3. <u>ASSURED PROMOTIONS.</u> Promotions are assured, as limitations for the administrator's actions become almost non-existent.

<u>DISADVANTAGES:</u>

1. <u>ENCROACHMENT.</u> Nobody is perfect. The administrator will sometimes encroach on the boss's authority of position. However, the administrator's authority of personality will quickly adjust his position to a proper perspective.

2. <u>PEER DISAPPROVAL.</u> The administrator's visible progress will appear over-aggressive. This will cause peers to disapprove his "rocking the boat." However, the administrator will accept unpopularity as the price to pay in competing for the next higher job.

<u>ACTION:</u> Begin today by developing a clear and solid viewpoint on Authority's two frames of reference . . . Responsibility and Accountability.

Chapter 12

How to Hack a Way Out of the Clerical Jungle

"When persistence toward well-designed goals is carried to the extreme, the individual will succeed."

INTRODUCTION: S. P. "Spotty" Inkwell, a department head at Unnorris College, brooded. "I'll be a department head all my life, if I stay at Unnorris. Think I'd better start looking for another job."

How come, Spotty? Aren't you happy in your work?

"Oh, the work's all right. It's just that I'll never get anywhere here. There's simply no way to get any attention."

What have you done that deserves attention?

"Well, I had an idea. And I wrote it down, did a Soppada on it. Then I went to see L. Patrick."

Who's L. Patrick?

"L. Pat, Dean of the College. Reports to Octangle Zooly. Ox Zooly is vice president and he runs the college when the president isn't here."

Okay. Continue.

"Well, I went in to see L. Pat. Presented my Soppada. He didn't even listen all the way through. Interrupted. Said Ox would never go for it. And he kind of implied I'd better not rock the boat. So I thought I'd best update my resume and find another boat."

You're free to do that, of course. But chances are you'll find the same resistance everywhere you go. Consider these two points, Spotty:

1. You're already here. You're familiar with the routines. You know the people. A man's best opportunity to succeed is, mostly, where he is.
2. If your ideas are good, and I assume they aren't all bad... then a high degree of persistence will get audiences for your ideas.

"But point number two is wrong. And that makes point number one wrong. That's what I was telling you."

I know what you were telling me. And what I'm telling you is that there is a way to get attention. There is a way to hack yourself a path out of the clerical jungle, up the success ladder.

"What's the way? Tell me."

Persistence.

"Persistence?"

Yes, persistence. With five steps. And those steps are:

1. Jot down many ideas
2. Flesh out all ideas
3. Make oral sales presentations at every opportunity
4. Persist beyond "normal" approaches
5. Get a reputation

12.1 JOT DOWN MANY IDEAS

Ideas come to all people. When this happens to you, Spotty, just make a note, a few words . . . enough so that, later, you can recall the idea you had. The alternative (and, unhappily, too many people let this alternative happen) is to file the idea mentally. Bad move. Because that idea may never recur.

"You're right about that. I can remember having ideas . . . but can't remember what they were."

Exactly. And those ideas may have blossomed into real plusses. But they won't, not now. They're lost. And they needn't be. Do this, Spotty:

1. When that idea hits, jot a few guiding comments on a piece of paper. Takes only a few seconds.
2. Put that piece of paper in your pocket, or in your desk.
3. At a time when you have decided to begin hatching your creative eggs, pull out those pieces of paper. You are now ready to begin Step Number Two.

12.2   FLESH OUT ALL IDEAS

As you find time, Spotty . . . and a man does manage to find time to improve himself . . . go to the privacy of your room, with those notes of your ideas. Select the one you feel you'd like to activate first. Create a "Soppada" on that idea.

You know, of course, Spotty . . . that Soppada is policy here at Unnorris College. All employees are encouraged to learn Soppada.

"'Encouraged' is right. As I recall Dr. Unnorris' announcement, he said something like . . . 'Anyone around here doesn't learn Soppada gets his behind booted by the head honcho . . . me.'"

That's fairly accurate. Dr. Unnorris is rather forcible. Anyway, you might run over Soppada again, Spotty. It's the fourth chapter in this book.

"Okay. Will do."

When you have created your Soppada, you'll have fleshed out your idea. It'll be there, on paper, in all its seven elements. And now you're ready for Step Number Three.

12.3 MAKE ORAL SALES PRESENTATIONS AT EVERY OPPORTUNITY

Spotty, here's your problem: Your target is L. Pat. An evasive target he is, too. He just doesn't seem at all ready to consider your idea. Yet, you can't go over his head and pitch Ox Zooly. That would be bad organization, bad politics . . .and you'd be hurt, in the long run. So . . . sell L. Pat.

Sure, you've already been turned down. But consider two things:

1. You were not turned down on logic. Until logic defeats your thinking, persist.
2. Your pitch was not professional. Whatever you presented . . . even if you had a Soppada . . . your pitch didn't get attention.

Now keep your Soppada with you. In your pocket. At times when L. Pat is nearby, present your Soppada orally. Even though he keeps turning you down, keep pitching. Even though he becomes exasperated with you, keep pitching. Even if he threatens to fire you, keep pitching.

You won't get fired, Spotty. Nobody gets fired for presenting ideas. Keep pitching. And be ready for even more threats and admonitions, as you move into Step Number Four.

12.4   PERSIST BEYOND "NORMAL" APPROACHES

As you get toward the end of Step Number Three, Spotty . . . you have already persisted beyond what normal and average people would do. But it takes still more, much more . . . if you are to succeed in your attack to get the attention of mahogany row.

Keep hammering on L. Pat, at every opportunity . . . to get him to pass your idea along. And, while you are hammering, develop other Soppadas from your other ideas. Be hammering L. Pat with two . . . three . . . four . . . or more . . . Soppadas. If L. Pat is a stand-pat guy, and he may very well be . . . keep hitting him head-on anyway.

Persist far beyond the point where average men would go. Far beyond. Be a pest. Be a nuisance. Persist. To the degree that you can, Spotty . . . ignore his howls of anguish . . . breast his threats . . . stand firm to his admonitions. Persist. Hardly anyone else would go this far. Hardly anyone else would manifest such firm beliefs in unshakable convictions. Persist.

While you are persisting, there are ways you can go over L. Pat's head . . . without violating rules of organization. Let's tick off one of the ways you can get top-level attention and still "be in line." It's called: "First you must get their attention."

1. Get a manila folder. On the front, in big felt-penned words, write: "PROGRESS-CAUSING IDEAS FOR UNNORRIS COLLEGE."

2. Place your Soppadas in the manila folder.

3. Place the manila folder on the corner of your desk nearest the aisle. That's where people will see the folder as they are walking through.

4. L. Pat may see the folder. Ox Zooly may see it. Indeed, Dr. Unnorris may see that folder. He roams frequently, and he misses very little.

5. If L. Pat sees your folder, he will surely be disturbed. But he can hardly ask you to not have progress-causing ideas.

    "What's that? What's that folder?"

    "Progress-causing ideas, L. Pat."

    "I keep it there so I can conveniently add more ideas. Why? Shouldn't I? Should I stop having ideas?"

    "Hey, Spotty . . . I didn't say that."

    "Okay, L. Pat. Thank you."

6. If Ox Zooly sees your folder, he'll be curious. He'll ask you about it.

    "What's that? What's that folder?"

"Progress-causing ideas, Dr. Zooly."

"What's it doing there?"

"I keep it there so I can conveniently add more ideas. I have quite a few already."

"Why don't I know about this?"

"Well, I must get by L. Pat first. When I do, you'll know."

"Have you tried, Spotty?"

"Well . . . yes."

"And . . . . . ?"

"I'll keep trying, Dr. Zooly."

"Good. But let's talk about your ideas anyway."

7. If Dr. Unnorris sees your folder, his eyes will light up like he has his tongue in the light socket. The word "progress" has a strong positive effect on Dr. Unnorris.

"What the heck is that? What the heck is in that folder? Says 'progress'."

"Those are progress-causing ideas, Dr. Unnorris . . . ways I feel our college can make more progress at less cost."

"Tell me about them. I want to know about making more progress."

"Well, I should go through the chain of command, Dr. Unnorris. Perhaps, when I do, they'll like my ideas."

"To heck with the chain of command. You tell me what you think and you tell me now."

8. Or you can stand by the water cooler, shaking your head . . . with a frustrated look on your face. When someone asks why you look ill, reply that you just can't squeeze another bit of progress from your new idea. The grapevine will then go to work, leading to your making the pitch.

9. Other means will come to you. Use them, if you must. But only when "original persistence" fails.

Now you ease into Step Number Five, Spotty.

12.5 GET A REPUTATION

As you persist far beyond the boundaries set by most men, Spotty . . . you will develop a reputation. On the surface, that reputation won't appear to be a good one. But it is a good reputation, when you consider three points:

1. People on or below your own level will view you with grudging admiration. They won't like

you, mind you . . . because you are venturing to succeed beyond their own potentials. But they will admire you and, later, will be good subordinates to you . . . when they work for you. Which they will.

2. People one and two levels above you will view you as a distinct threat. They will dislike you heartily. More than that. To the degree that they are able, these men will work against you.

But they will not succeed. The saying "You can't keep a good man down" is no tired cliché. And here's a warning, Spotty: While the men one and two levels above you, L. Patrick Semicut and Octangle Zooly, will not destroy your progress . . . they'll probably come pretty close. So, while you are hacking your way out of the clerical jungle, go to great lengths to cooperate with L. Pat and Ox.

You won't win them over. But you might advance from "active resistance" to "passive dislike" by then.

3. The top man, Dr. Unnorris . . . now, he'll like you, Spotty. Very likely it will take some while for Dr. Unnorris to get the word about what you are up to. But, in time, word of your aggressive approaches, toward college progress and personal success, will get to the top guy. When that happens, you'll have the strongest push an aspiring administrator can get: the pleasure of the head honcho.

12.6   THE ACHIEVING ACTION

Persistence alone does not guarantee success. When persistence is pigheaded pursuit of doubtful causes and half-baked ideas, then persistence can be deadly.

But when persistence promotes solid thinking and discernible progress . . . and when that persistence is carried far beyond the puny efforts of average men . . . then persistence becomes a hard and fast foothold for the individual whose dedication to success is a deep and much desired goal.

Persist. Hang in. Persist.

SUCCESS EXERCISES

After having studied Chapter 12 you should be able to:

(1) Persist toward well-designed goals to the degree and extent that success will occur . . . your own individual success

12-1   On a piece of paper "flesh-out" ideas that when implemented will increase your college's progress-line . . . ideas that will make your job go better.

12-2   Choose your best idea of Exercise 12-1. Write it in the SOPPADA format.

12-3   Plan an oral presentation around your SOPPADA. Make your pitch. Leave a copy of the SOPPADA . . . and suggest a future discussion date. Persist to the extreme.

12-4   Begin developing a SOPPADA folder. As ideas occur write them into SOPPADA form. As opportunities occur make your pitch on a particular SOPPADA. Store your folder on the corner of your desk "nearest to the boss's office." Curiosity will get the best of him . . . then do persist!

About The Author

Dr. Wayne Scott is an acclaimed consultant, author, and internationally-known platform speaker. He received his Ph.D. from The Ohio State University and is also a graduate of Harvard University's Institute for Educational Management, The University of North Carolina's School of Business Executive Development Program, and The American Management Association's President Institute and Management Course.

During the past twenty years, Dr. Scott has served as a Senior Lecturer and Chairperson for The American Management Associations. He has served as a college president at DeKalb College and Gaston College. He has authored numerous articles, publications, and books on human motivation, self-directed behavioral change, and leadership. Dr. Scott currently serves as the Chief Executive Officer at the Covington-Newton campus of DeKalb Technical College.

9 781588 201324